Contributions

Please send your tax deductible check to:

WORLD-WIDE MISSIONS OUTREACH
Dr. Jerry & Normadeene Gibson
11108 East Quartet Ave.
Mesa, AZ 85212

7.5 % profit from the sales of this book will be given to charities for missions and to help the poor.

Love is like a Lizard

THE AUTOBIOGRAPHY OF A CHRISTIAN MISSIONARY

AND HIS WORK OF MENTORING IN AMERICA

BY

DR. JERRY GIBSON

Burning Daylight

Copyright © 2012 by Jerry Gibson. All rights reserved.

Published by Burning Daylight an imprint of
Pearn and Associates, Inc.
1600 Edora Court Suite D
Fort Collins, Colorado 80525
For our submission guidelines please
contact happypoet@hotmail.com.

Cover design by Anne Kilgore. Photos with permission of Dr. Jerry Gibson

Library of Congress Control Number: 2011943513

Gibson, Jerry
Love is like a Lizard, by Dr. Jerry Gibson.
First edition.

ISBN 978-0-9846523-2-7 paper

PRINTED IN THE UNITED STATES OF AMERICA
Canada, United Kingdom, Europe, and Australia

First edition

DEDICATION AND ACKNOWLEDGEMENTS

We want to begin by acknowledging Barbara Schuler was my secretary when we came to the Boulder Valley Christian Church. She was the Executive Secretary for the Boulder Valley Christian Church. She helped us establish a bank account and used The Boulder Valley Christian Church as our covering before we were a recognized non-profit Christian organization. We received our Certificate of Incorporation as a nonprofit religious organization from the State of Colorado on August 31, 1989. She wrote letters and faithfully served our every need. We will be forever indebted to her for the way she helped us get started in our mission.

We also want to recognize the faithful Board of Advisors members for World-Wide Missions Outreach. Some of them have been with our mission from its inception.

Everett and Paula Ford served on our board in the first year of our mission. They supported our mission financially and opened their home — hosting our first board meetings. Paula also put together our first newsletters. Without their love and support, we would have had a very difficult time getting started.

John and Virginia Arvidson as well as Michael and Sherlene Howard were also very valuable members of our Board of Advisors.

As we write this book, our Board of Advisors consists of Hal and Jan Riggs, Doug and Beth Keasling and Richard and Judy Bussman who have been with World-Wide Missions Outreach from the beginning. They have been faithful counselors, but more important, faithful friends. Words cannot adequately express how much they have contributed to the success of World-Wide Missions Outreach's ministry, as well as to the overall content of this book.

There are hundreds of people whose names, for practical reasons, we will not mention, who have supported World-Wide Missions Outreach with regular financial contributions that deserve recognition. There are also many churches that have done the same. A simple thank you hardly seems adequate. However, we do want to express our gratitude toward them all.

CONTENTS

Dedication and Acknowledgments *v*

Author's Note: Writing About Mentoring *ix*

Foreword *xv*

Preface *xvii*

Money Left by our Angel 1

The Adventure Began 8

Boulder Men's Christian Fellowship 12

The Fellowship of Christian Fire Fighters 22

The Fellowship of Christian Athletes 26

A Bittersweet Revelation 29

Christian Student Fellowship Booth at the UMC 34

International Students 44

Jerry's Gems — Standley Lake High School 46

From Boulder Valley Christian Church to World-Wide Missions Outreach 55

Mentoring Mentors 61

Proof of Perfection 70

Mentoring for Marriage 74

Our Legacy 81

Angels in England 90

Those Amazing Twenty-three Years 95

The Last Hurrah 96

The Fruit of our Labor 97

Photos of Some of the Men and Women Who Were Baptized 102

Bible Quiz Answers 105

AUTHOR'S NOTE, WRITING ABOUT MENTORING

Several people whom I asked to read over the material in this book commented that what I have presented is disjointed and lacks continuity. Therefore I deem it necessary to explain where I am coming from and why seemingly the lack of continuity is built into the experiences I am attempting to share with the reader.

Everything that I have done in the past has worked together to prepare me for the ministry I am having today. I will go back as far as my memory will recall to demonstrate how one's past experiences have a profound effect on all that follows. I must begin with many of the things I shared in my first published book, *Worth Any Sacrifice.*

Being born in Jacksonville, Florida in 1926 into a family of a wonderful mother and father and three very talented older sisters was a wonderful way to begin my life's journey. The fact that my father was a physical education major in college pretty much predicted what he would have to do to earn a living. Six of us left Florida and headed north to Minnesota where Dad became involved in the physical education program of Minneapolis. Our family of four soon became a family of ten. The Great Depression hit at a time when Father had taken time to become an excellent dance teacher. This served to put food on our table during the difficult summer months when Dad was not teaching school. Dad used our entire family to promote his dancing career. We became "The Gibson Review" and traveled to County Fairs throughout Minnesota and Wisconsin to sport his wares. Somehow, my nature rebelled against anything that had to do with dancing. Due to my negative attitude, I was soon dropped from "The Gibson Review's core of dancers.

In my early teens I was able to walk to the Minnetonka Country Club, near Excelsior, Minnesota, and earn money to help keep food on our table, by becoming a caddy. I worked hard at my newly found profession and ended up by becoming an "Honor Caddy." This gave me more money for carrying golf bags along with other special privileges. One of them that stand out in my mind was being chosen to caddy for the famous "Triple Crown Winner," Walter Hagan and his son, when they came to play an exhibition round of golf at Minnetonka Country Club.

The most influential person in my life during that very important informative age was not my birth father. He was Bruce Reinecker, the Club Champion. Bruce and his brothers founded National School Studios, which became a multi-million dollar business that specialized in taking school pictures for high schools. We became very close friends. He treated me more like the son he never had, than a poor little caddy from a family of ten. Several times he suggested he would like to adopt me away from my parents so he could give me some advantages my parents were unable to afford. He taught me how to play golf, which led to my winning the First Flight Caddy Championship at Minnetonka Country Club when I was twelve years old. With this background I was instrumental in establishing Golf Teams in two high schools that I attended before joining the navy in 1943 in the midst of the Second World War. I was only a junior in high school at the time, but felt an urgency to join many of my high school friends who were already on active duty. I failed to mention that due to our family's frequent moving from house to house when I was very young, I had to repeat the Third Grade. This had a devastating affect on my self-esteem. I can still hear my older sister's voices as they teased me, "Junior failed! Junior Failed!" I am sure my sisters did not mean me any harm, yet without realizing it, they were being very cruel. To this day, I can still feel the affect of that teasing, as I have a difficult time not being defensive in regard to many of the things that I have done.

My experience as an Aviation Electronic Technician in the United States Navy during the Second World War had an impact on what was to follow. My experience as a student in a secular college in California, where I had the honor of being the captain of a championship golf team, played an important roll in my life.

My conversion experience, that led me to Minnesota Bible College where I met my wife of more than sixty years, Normadeene, had a tremendous impact on all that follows. Founding a new church, while I was still in Bible College, further prepared me for my ministry. I might better say, "us," rather than "me," for from the time I met and married Normadeene, we have worked as a team. Our accepting the call to be the minister of The Youngstown Christian Church in Youngstown, Illinois that led to my Enrolling in Lincoln Bible Institute and Lincoln Christian Seminary, where I received the better part of my upper level education, prepared me for opportunities of Christian service that would have otherwise been impossible, is also reflected in the pages of this book. Taking a denominational church with all of its extra-Biblical teachings and helping to lead them to become a simple non-denominational Christian Church is indelibly inscribed into the pages of this book. Becoming a full time professor at Minnesota Bible College where we were also instrumental in establishing several churches in the Minneapolis area, as well as pioneering in the establishment of a campus ministry at the University of Minnesota. At the same time, I was afforded the privilege of serving on the staff of the Dean of Students, as well as the Counsel of Religious Advisors of that great university.

After ten years of teaching, Minnesota Bible College afforded me a Sabbatical Leave. I had the opportunity to go to Israel as part of a team that was led by a professor from a nearby college to help decipher the Dead Sea Scrolls. Even though I had my heart set on being a part of that mission, God had different ideas for us. We were called to Ghana, West Africa to establish a Christian College. That college today has been awarded the status of a university. That experience prepared us for much of what was to follow that I have attempted to recount in this book. Through a series of strange situations, we accepted the call to the campus ministry at the University of Illinois. We arrived there during the time of campus unrest, with the Kent State tragedy having a tremendous effect on our ministry there. I was elected to be the Secretary for "University Professors for Academic Order. At the same time I was given an Academic Appointment from the Board of Regents of the University of Illinois to teach Religious Studies classes as part of the elective curriculum of the university. I also became a part of the staff of the Dean of Students, just as I had served at the University of Minnesota. It was there that I met, through rather strange fortunes, Byron Tarr from Liberia which led to our missionary journey to Liberia where we established Liberia Christian College. The college was served by Charles Boatman, Wayne Meece and others from America. Also, Abba Karnga, from Liberia. This did a great deal to further prepare us for the work with international students, which also had an integral part in the writing of this book. Becoming the Senior Minister of the Webber Street Church in Urbana, Illinois gave us further experience that has served us well in the years to follow. Accepting the call to the presidency of Mid-South Christian College in Senatobia, Mississippi, rather than accepting the call to be a professor at Ozark Bible College in Joplin Missouri, was a "cross roads" decision that helped to make possible much of what is shared in these pages. The most important decision of all, however, was our decision to leave Mid-South Christian College, which at that time had moved to Memphis, Tennessee, and establish World-Wide Missions Outreach with the help of the faithful men and women on our board, more than twenty years ago. All of the above experiences and ministries are woven into the pages of this book. Understanding that fact will help you see that there is continuity; even though the presentation may seem disjointed. I beg of you, please be patient and wait until we come to the final pages before you pass judgment as to its value as a tool to help prepare Mentors of Mentors.

FOREWORD

Love is like a Lizard my book about mentoring mentors may well be considered a sequel to the great faith chapter in the New Testament, Hebrews eleven or *Plutarch's Lives*. We are in no way inferring that we are in any way on a par with the men and women listed in that remarkable catalogue of faithful Bible characters. The main similarity is the fact that God answered our simple prayers of faith, in the same way He did all through the Bible, and demonstrated the fact that we can do, what we know we cannot do, with the help of God.

There is no way possible for Normadeene and I to have established World-Wide Missions Outreach, with the help of our faithful board members, without what I believe to have been direct Divine intervention. We believe you will agree with that assessment as you follow the narrative of *Love is like a Lizard*.

The primary purpose in writing this book is to inspire the reader to not be satisfied with being what the Apostle Paul calls, *walking like mere men, I Corinthians 3:3*. We desire to challenge you to make a commitment to be a part of an adventure in faith that will pay you rewards and give you the satisfaction of achievement like nothing else can do. We are talking about preparing yourself to be a Mentor of Mentors.

When you become a Mentor of Mentors, your legacy in the lives of the people you mentor and prepare to be mentors will be legion. For if they are true to their commitment of being a mentor or disciple maker, by the time their lives have run their course, they will have influenced a multiplication table of mentors as their legacy who are your legacy, too.

PREFACE

We have shared the first sixty years of our pilgrimage in our first three books: *Worth Any Sacrifice; Angels in Africa;* and *Time For One More Play.* This book will wear the title *Love is like a Lizard,* and cover the topic of mentoring mentors due to the fact we have spent most of our sixty years of ministry mentoring both the young, and the old men and women, from every walk of life. It will cover close to the last twenty-three years of our lives.

You may recall, if you have read *Angels In Africa,* when I attended the University of Ghana, being the only white person in the midst of several hundred black men and women, I was greeted with a loud "Ho brunie!" Or, "Ho white man!" as I entered the assembly hall where the classes were being conducted. Also, on one occasion, the chief of one of the villages, in an attempt to make me feel comfortable, compared me to the white keys on a piano. He exclaimed how both the white and black keys were necessary in order to produce the best quality of sound. On another occasion the person who introduced me expounded, "Professor Gibson may be white, but his heart is just as black as ours!" We have enjoyed a chuckle over that through the years.

I was invited to speak at Montebello High School in Denver, Colorado. The plan was for me to answer questions from the freshmen, sophomore, junior and senior classes, each for an hour from 10:00 a.m. in the morning until 2:00 p.m. in the afternoon. The opportunity was made possible by Albus Brooks, whom I mentored when he was attending the University of Colorado. He was, and still is, at the time of this writing, the director for the Central Denver Area Young Life ministry. Montebello High School consists of nearly ninety percent black students. I was accompanied by Normadeene as well as Hong and Song from South Korea. Hong and Song had never been to a high school in America and were eager to do so.

As Albus surveyed the situation, he wondered if I would be able to communicate with the black students who he thought presented an almost impossible cultural gap for me. He contemplated as to how he should introduce me. He stood up and announced, "I want to introduce you to an old white man." That helped inspire me while I was writing *Love is like a Lizard*. Many of those types of events have continued to inspire me to write all four of my books.

We will skip over the seven years we spent in Senatobia, Mississippi as President of Mid-South Christian College; however, the circumstances surrounding our leaving there had a bearing on our move to Colorado.

I do want to mention though, that the faculty and staff we worked with at Mid-South Christian College was the finest we could put together. Mark and Ann Fessler as well as Rob and Kathy Smith, made a tremendous contribution to both the academic and social atmosphere of the college before they took positions in Georgia and Missouri respectively. When we moved to Colorado, we left the college in capable hands. Bill Griffin and Bob Secrist served well as the Administrative Staff. Tim and Terrell Viner, Vernon and Denni Eaton, Bill and Jonie Baker, Steve and Jenny Clotfelter, and David and Virginia Savage were excellent in the classroom.

It is our belief that the years we spent at Mid-South Christian College served to help prepare us for our ministry in Colorado. We believe that our time was well spent, as it served as a source of salvation for our daughter, Cindy, and our granddaughter, Missy, as they needed a place to live after a crisis experience with Cindy's husband, Kenny Derouen. He was killed in a boating accident in the Gulf of Mexico. Cindy was the Food Service Manager for the College while we were there.

We gained many lasting friends from the Mid-South area with whom we have kept in close touch since moving to Colorado. We are confident that we have a lasting legacy in the lives of both students and faculty of the College, as well as many of the churches we ministered to while we were there. Someday we may author a book written specifically to recount our experiences there.

As I contemplate the content of this book as to what I have written up until this time, I have come to the conclusion that I actually have two books in one. The first half of the book deals with the seemingly impossible circumstances that led to our ministry for the past twenty years. The last half of the book deals with the actual function of our mentoring ministry as well as the basic teaching materials we have used in our mentoring of mentors. A careful editing was done by my long time friend and former student, Robert Mignealt.

MONEY LEFT BY OUR ANGEL

It was a cold, blustery Thursday in December of 1987 when we left Mississippi to drive to Boulder, Colorado. Lack of cash flow to administer the affairs of Mid-South Christian College forced me to tender my resignation as its President. We negotiated the sale of the College's property in Mississippi and purchased a beautiful campus next to Graceland in Memphis. Unfortunately, our negotiations for the sale of the Mississippi property failed. That left us with two large mortgages of well over a million dollars. The interest on our debt was more than we could pay. We managed to pay the salaries of our faculty and staff, most of who had relocated in Memphis, but were not able to provide a salary for myself. Due to having excellent credit, Normadeene and I managed to live off of our bank cards for a few months, but were only able to pay the interest on them, and were borrowing money to pay for that.

We contacted several prospective opportunities for ministry. We long had a desire to locate back in a university town as we had a keen interest in the campus ministry. We had a special interest in working with International Students. Our experience with Internationals at the University of Minnesota, and my experience with International Students in Ghana, and our further experience with them at the University of Illinois, convinced us that the university campus was the ideal place to prepare foreign missionaries. Our desire was to reach Internationals for Christ in America, train them, and send them back as missionaries to their own people. We did not realize we were destined to have an experience with angels similar to what we had experienced in Ghana, West Africa, twenty-two years earlier.

Earl and Virginia Justice, two of my former students, had located in Boulder, Colorado and were serving The Boulder Valley Christian Church. Earl was the Senior Minister there. He advised us of the excellent opportunity afforded us at The University of Colorado in Boulder. He said there were more Internationals there than on any other campus in America. He said he would set up a meeting with his elders on Saturday morning December 12, 1987, and have me preach at the Boulder Valley Christian Church on Sunday morning. He advised us that the church most likely would not offer us any immediate financial support, but would provide us with an office and covering for our new ministry. At that time we had not yet decided on a name for our mission. We immediately sent out letters to former students and friends asking for their prayers and financial support. We stressed the urgency of our need as we had resigned from Mid-South Christian College effective January 8, 1988. We especially needed help for our moving expenses. At the time we felt that was our greatest prayer need.

We arrived in Boulder, Colorado, early Friday morning on the 11th of December and drove directly to the Boulder Valley Christian Church on 5300 Baseline Road. We were immediately shaken by the news that Earl Justice had failed to notify his elders of our coming. He hurriedly arranged a Saturday morning breakfast meeting for us with his elders at Karen's Kitchen in Louisville. We had no idea what to expect. We started to have second thoughts about the wisdom of our moving to Colorado.

We were greeted cordially, but rather coldly, by the elders of the Boulder Valley Church the next morning at Karen's Kitchen. They wanted to know why we were there. They seemed to be rather suspicious of our motives. They wanted to know why we were leaving Mid-South Christian College. I could see and feel by the look on Normadeene's face that she was very disappointed that the elders had not been informed of our coming. They insisted from the very beginning of our meeting that they would not be able to give us any financial support, and even though they would be willing to provide an office for us, that would only be after they heard my presentation to the church on Sunday morning.

We left the meeting with an unsettled feeling in our stomachs. I quoted over and over in my mind the words of the Apostle Paul in II Timothy 1: 7, "*We have not been given the spirit of fear, but of power, love and self-control.*" Also, I Corinthians 10:13 was a source of great comfort where Paul writes, "*There has no temptation taken you but what is common to man; and God is faithful, who will not allow you to be tempted or tried beyond what you are able, but will also with the temptation provide a way of escape, that you will be able to bear it.*" God has never failed us in His promises. We knew we be able to put that promise in the bank and count on it.

That afternoon, we looked through the Want Ads in the Daily Camera, Boulder's main newspaper, for possible places to live. We found that rent in Boulder was far too expensive for our prospective budget, so looked to surrounding communities. We found an ad for an apartment in Louisville, not far from where we had met for breakfast. We drove out to Louisville and located the apartment behind the Safeway grocery store. There was no garage, and it had only two bedrooms. We wondered how we would manage all of my books, as well as the furniture we had accumulated through the years, in such a small apartment. We decided we could most likely find a storage locker until we could manage a larger place to live.

We had drawn up a temporary budget, based on the cost of things in Mississippi. We allotted $550.00 per month for rent. We thought that was all we would be able to pay until we raised our base of financial support. The lady who was in charge of renting the apartment said that the rent was $600.00 per month. When we explained to her our circumstances, she agreed to let us have it for $550.00 if we would rent it starting on the first of January, and also put down a two month's deposit of $1,100.00. We agreed to do so, but told her we could not close with her until after I preached on Sunday morning, as we did not know for sure we would be able to move to Colorado. She agreed to hold the apartment for us until Sunday afternoon. We had no idea where the $1,100.00 deposit would come from.

Sunday morning, the 13th day of December, was a different story. It seemed the Lord prepared the way for us. We were received warmly by the congregation. We also could sense the elders were thawing out and changing their minds from their first impressions. We could sense an air of excitement and great expectations permeating the sanctuary as I presented our dreams for our mission.

When I left the pulpit I was approached by the Chairman of the elders and told us we would be more than welcome to locate our mission in the church building and would be provided an office out of which to work. However, I was reminded once again the church would not be able to provide us any financial assistance.

Before we came to Boulder, the church had provided a house for Leland Griffin, who was working as a Counselor for them. He had recently resigned from that position, and was moving from the house. The church was paying $900.00 per month rent to one of its members, Steve Taniguchi. We were told it would be an ideal place for us to live. We could not see how we could possibly pay that much rent.

As we walked down the isle toward the back of the church, we were approached by Steve Taniguchi. He inquired, "I hear you are looking for a place to live, how about my house in Lafayette?" I replied, "We would love to be able to live in your house, but there is no way we can afford to pay the rent the church has been paying you. In fact, we are on our way out to Louisville to close the deal on an apartment we plan to rent until we get on our feet and can afford a place like yours." He inquired, "How much are you going to pay for the apartment in Louisville?" I told him, "$550.00. To that he responded, "You can have my house for $550.00 per month. After hearing you this morning, I am convinced God wants me to be in partnership with you and your mission. It is yours for $550.00 per month." God's strong hand was indeed upon us. This was one of the first signs that convinced us that God wanted us to be in Colorado.

Before leaving for Colorado, by faith, we had arranged to have our furniture and belongings moved from Mississippi to Colorado. The estimated cost for the move was approximately $4,000.00. The moving company was waiting for us to confirm their moving us when we got back from Colorado. We now had to worry about how we would come up with $4000.00. They would not take anything but a certified check for their services.

We left early on Monday morning to return to Mississippi. On the way home we ran into a full-blown blizzard between Wichita and Topeka. The only way we were able to stay on the road was to follow closely behind a large trailer-truck, which we believe was an "angel-semi," since there was nobody else on the snow-covered highway but us. We arrived in Topeka late at night completely exhausted, but very thankful for our "angel-semi" that had guided us safely to a motel that night.

We arrived back in Senatobia, Mississippi, late on Tuesday afternoon. On the way home we decided on the name "World-Wide Missions Outreach" for our mission. We got the inspiration for that name due to our keen interest in working with Internationals as previously mentioned. Also, from to our rather new interest in working with Chinese students because we were told there was a large population of Chinese students on the University of Colorado campus. We thought China was most likely the country Isaiah 54: 1-3 was referring to. For China at that time boasted a population of one billion two hundred million people. We came up with an idea for our logo that would highlight the fact that "It is no farther to heaven from Beijing, China, than from Boulder, Colorado." As you will see, this proved to be providential. To this day that logo is on our letter head and other documents.

Shortly after arriving back home in Mississippi, we received a phone call from Earl Justice. He informed us that a very wonderful thing had happened. He said when Barbara Schuler opened the door to the church offices on Monday morning, she found an envelope addressed to Jerry and Normadeene Gibson. Upon opening it, she found it contained twenty-five new one hundred dollar bills. There was a note saying it was for Jerry and Normadeene's moving expenses. To this day nobody knows where it came from, that is, nobody but Normadeene and I. We immediately remembered the bank in Kumasi where our angel left us a bank draft for a thousand dollars. Once again our angel provided for a large part of our urgent need to pay the movers. When we opened our mail we found a check for $1,500.00 from Virgil and Laverne Marshall, two of our dear friends from Wymore, Nebraska to whom we had sent a letter asking for support of our new mission. They included a note with their check expressing their desire to help us with our moving expenses. We had our moving expenses taken care of! Now, all we had to do was raise the base support for World-Wide Missions Outreach. Once again, we fit the definition of missionaries because we were going where we had not been, to do what we had not done, with money we did not have. "Indeed, we walk by faith, and not by sight," II Corinthians 5: 7.

Here we are, twenty years later. Words cannot begin to express how much we appreciate the faithful, loving support of you, our Board of Advisors who have been with us from the beginning: Doug and Beth Keasling, Richard and Judy Bussmann, and Hal and Jan Riggs. You have stood by us and helped direct the path of our ministry in a way that demonstrated the fact that God's strong hand has been upon you. Your legacy for these past twenty years will produce many stars in your crowns. There is no way we can adequately thank you enough. However, we can give special recognition to you for what you have done to make the ministry of World-Wide Missions possible.

THE ADVENTURE BEGAN

Beacon Moving and Storage agreed to move us to Lafayette, Colorado for $4,000.00. God provided for the bank draft they required. We were then faced with the dilemma of raising a base of financial support for our new venture in Colorado. We worked out a budget, based on what we had learned during our visit to Boulder. We sent letters to those we had previously contacted, and added many more to that list. We realized it would take some time before we gained enough support to sustain our ministry. However, we were convinced that God wanted us in Colorado. We also firmly believed as we experienced in the past, God never calls us to a task in which He does not provide the means to accomplish that task. Once again, we were going where we had not been, to do what we had not done, with money we did not have. We knew that we could do what we knew we could not do, with the help of God. I have often counseled Christians who were confronted by seemingly impossible obstacles, "We must work as though all depends upon us, and pray as though all depends upon God." That has proven to be the formula for success for laborers in God's Vineyard.

We spent Christmas vacation packing books, pictures, along with other personal items we would carry to Colorado in our automobiles. I say automobiles, because we had two. We had a 1983 Chrysler New Yorker, and a 1985 Dodge. Both of them were equipped with CB's so we could keep in close communication as we caravanned our way to Colorado. Normadeene would lead the way in the Chrysler, as it was easier to drive and more mechanically sound. We were in for another adventure of a lifetime.

The movers packed and loaded the huge moving van and were leaving for Colorado the next morning. Normadeene and I attended a farewell get-together with the trustees and faculty, and staff of Mid South Christian College, and would also leave early the next morning. We did not sleep much that night. We had butterflies in our stomachs, as we still did not know how we could possibly survive the first few months in Colorado without more financial support for our mission. However, we managed to turn our concerns over to the Lord, and He provided the peace of mind we needed, at least, to get a little much needed rest. We had a long journey ahead of us.

We left Senatobia, Mississippi, early the morning of January 6th. We planned to drive as far as Dardanelle, Arkansas, where we would spend the night with our long-time friends, Del and Nancy McGehe. Del and Nancy were the hosts for my Pastor's class when I was the Senior Minister for the Webber Street Church of Christ in Urbana, Illinois. They had only recently moved there from Urbana.

Not far out of Memphis, it started to snow. By the time we arrived in Dardanelle, Interstate 40 had become snow-packed. People in that part of the Mid-south are not used to driving on slippery roads. We found ourselves digging our toenails into the floor boards of our vehicles in an attempt to stay on the highway. We moved at a snail's pace. We called Del from a gas station in Dardanelle. He told us to park our car. It was too dangerous for us to drive to his house. He agreed to come and get us with his pickup truck. By the time we arrived at Del and Nancy's home we were exhausted. It was a great relief to be in a warm house. Del and Nancy treated us like royalty. We had a lot of catching up to do, so we talked into the late hours of the night.

It seemed like we had just bid our hosts, "Goodnight," when the alarm went off and we needed to resume our journey to Colorado. Del and Nancy drove us back to Dardanelle where we thanked them and bid them farewell.

It had snowed all night. When we turned off the ramp onto Interstate 40, we could not see the lane markers. We agreed to keep in close touch via our CB radios, and also to drive very slowly. The only vehicles on the highway were large semi-tractor trailers. We could not see the highway, but managed to follow very close to a semi that led the way for us just like when we drove home from Wichita to Topeka on our way back home from Boulder.

It was a complete whiteout. We could not see more than a few feet in front of us, so we stayed as close as possible to the rear end of the semi. Normadeene had come down with a bad cold. Her nose needed wiping, but she did not dare take her hands off the steering wheel to wipe it. We literally slid into Oklahoma City late that night. We found a motel to stay in off of Interstate 35. We prayed without ceasing all of the way and thanked God for our CB radios. They were our only means of communication when we needed to stop for gas or other necessities. We were convinced our angels kept us from sliding into a ditch and kept us on the snow-packed, slippery highway.

We left early the next morning and managed to drive as far as Limon, Colorado. The roads were ice-covered as we took the ramp off of Interstate 70 to stay at a Motel 8 in Limon. We slid to a stop in front of the motel. We left early the next morning and arrived in Boulder around noon on January 8, 1988. We were there at last! As before, we drove directly to the Boulder Valley Christian Church and obtained a key to our house in Lafayette from Barb Schuler. She informed us that she had received a call from our movers. They had slid off the highway and were stuck in a snowdrift. They said they would not make it to Colorado for at least a couple more days. That meant we would have no beds to sleep on or any other household goods and would have to improvise until the movers got there.

We drove to Lafayette and entered our new home for the first time. There was a cozy little fireplace in the family room. The floors were all carpeted, so we agreed we would be able to sleep on the floor in front of the fireplace in the family room until our furniture arrived.

We drove into Boulder to the Crossroads Mall. There was a Montgomery Wards department store there. We decided to purchase a queen-size floor mattress. It would not only satisfy our immediate need for a bed to sleep on, but would also be very valuable when our children and grandchildren came to stay with us.

As I looked for things we might need, I noticed Normadeene talking to a very tall black man. She is very friendly, so I was not surprised. However, I *was* surprised when I joined them to hear the rather personal nature of their conversation. The young man was Cliff Mealy. He was a basketball star for the University of Colorado who went on to play in the NBA with both the Los Angeles Lakers and the Houston Oilers. He needed someone to talk to. It turned out to be love at fist sight. He sold us a very nice air mattress and gave us his telephone number and asked us to call him.

After we were settled in our new home, we invited him for dinner. He brought with him his girlfriend, Visha Sedlack, who was a world class race walker. We fell in love with her, also. They both started to attend the Boulder Valley Christian Church. We were destined to have some wonderful times of sweet fellowship with them in the months and years to follow.

THE BOULDER MEN'S CHRISTIAN FELLOWSHIP

We were more convinced than ever that we were in the right place at the right time. However, we still did not know how we were going to make both ends meet in regards to our financial situation. He did so for us in a way we never could have imagined. "Man proposes, but God disposes," we have said often.

I spent the first couple of weeks getting acquainted with the Boulder Valley Christian Church staff as well as orienting myself to the University of Colorado. At that time the BVCC staff consisted of Earl Justice, Senior minister, Douglas Chastain, Kathy Howe, and later Troy Justice as Youth Minister. John Morfue was serving as a campus minister. Bob Overholser was the custodian.

Friday morning, after we arrived in Colorado, Earl Justice invited me to attend an early Friday morning Flatirons Country Club prayer breakfast in Boulder. That proved to be one of the most significant experiences that helped to mold the direction of our new ministry. It also connects with what I will be sharing with you a little later in this book.

In 1982 there was a Fellowship of Christian Athletes meeting in Denver. Bill McCartney, the Head Football Coach for the University of Colorado, and Fisher DeBerry, an Assistant Coach for Ken Hatfield at the Air Force Academy, who later became the Head Football Coach at the Academy, were the speakers. Bill McCartney related that the thing he missed the most since moving from Michigan was an early Morning Prayer Breakfast with a group of men at a Sambo's Restaurant in Ann Arbor.

Darrell Baugh was there. He offered to get a group of men together and Bill quickly accepted. Darrell invited Dave Wardell, Will Rutlege and Fred Hendricks. With those men along with Bill and Darrell, there were five men at that first historic meeting. They met in Darrell's office every Friday morning at 6:30 a.m.

In the spring of 1983, Bill suggested they enlarge their group. Each of the original men invited five men to meet at the Flatiron's Country Club. Besides the speaker, Bo Mitchell, twelve men attended the first meeting. They were Bill McCartney, Will Rutlege, Dave Wardell, Fred Hendricks, Dan Stavely, Andy Bryant, John Randall, Jerry Gilkison, Don Coen, Phil Irwin, Hal Riggs and Darrell Baugh. They called themselves The Boulder Christian Men's Fellowship. I doubt if any of them realized at the time what a tremendous impact that group of men would make on the Boulder community, as on the rest of the world.

At the first meeting I attended at Flatirons Country Club, I met men who would make a lasting contribution to my Christian walk. One of them was army Colonel Hal Riggs, who became Normadeene's and my best friend, along with his wife, Jan. He helped Doug Chastain, Earl Justice son-in law, get a job selling automobiles for Pollard's Pontiac. I believe Doug introduced me to Hal. Jan and Hal later became charter members of the Board of Directors for World-Wide Missions Outreach. I also was introduced to John Arvidson, who along with his wife, Virginia became our close friends. John was one of World-Wide Mission's very first Board Chairman.

The format for the Friday morning meetings was to introduce and welcome new faces, followed by an opening prayer. That was followed by a lively songfest led by the talented Will Rutlege who was able to make the piano talk. At first, that was followed by a time of prayer requests. This time of prayer proved to be the call to fame of this group of men. The men would bare their souls with their heart-rending requests in behalf of the urgent needs in their lives. This often ran over into the time allotted the speaker, so it was moved to the end of the meeting. It was then time for a special guest speaker who would attempt to challenge the men *"to walk worthy of the vocation for which they were called."* Ephesians 4: l. It was, and still is, a truly non-denominational approach to Christianity. Men and women from every denominational background were invited to speak. I had the privilege to address the men on several occasions.

Due to extenuating circumstance, the breakfast meeting was moved to Second Baptist Church. Boulder Valley Christian Church relocated to South Boulder Road, and Second Baptist Church purchased their old building at 5300 Baseline Road.

* * *

I would not consider myself to be a *Calvinist* in my theological views. I do not limit the power of God in any way. However, I believe many Christians confuse the word *predestination* with *foreknowledge.* I have always believed salvation was made possible on Calvary, but not inevitable. God limited Himself when He made man a free moral agent. He gave man the intelligence to consider the consequence of his actions. In doing so, He made man both accountable and responsible for his actions. That is what makes man different from an animal. An animal is a conscious being. Man is a self-conscious being. Once again, salvation was predestined by God through the death of Jesus Christ on the cross *"before the foundation of the world was framed,*" Revelation 13: 8. It was predestined that, everyone who accepts Jesus Christ as Lord and Savior by faith will be saved, John 3: 16. We are predestined for service, but not for salvation. Salvation is conditioned on one's own free will. Noah Webster, the man who gave us the dictionary, said that the fact of man's being both responsible and accountable was his most important realization in life.

You may wonder why I went into such great detail to explain my position in regard to *Calvinism* theology. It is due to the fact that I believe strongly in *Divine Providence.* "Man proposes, but it is God who disposes" comes from that belief. What many people consider to be *luck* or coincidence, I believe to be *providence*. I have often commented that being *lucky* is a matter of being prepared when an avenue of opportunity is opened up to you. What follows is what I believe to be *the providence of God.*

In the late nineteen-seventies, our youngest son, G.A., moved to the Detroit, Michigan, area to take a position in a shopping center clothing store in the suburb of Macomb. At the same time, two of the young men who we mentored at the University of Illinois, Jeff and Mark Hollenbach, took jobs in Ann Arbor at the Play Maker shoe store which was owned and operated by a mutual friend, Maurie Daigneau. Shortly after arriving there, the Hollenbach brothers were introduced to a prayer breakfast at a Sambo's Restaurant in Taylor organized by an assistant Coach from the University of Michigan's football team whose name was Bill McCartney. He drove every Tuesday morning from Ann Arbor to Taylor, where they held a prayer breakfast at the local Sambo's because Sambo's was always packed full of men from off of the street, from every walk of life, would meet on a weekly basis at 6:15 a.m. for prayer and devotions as well as a message from an inspirational speaker. That speaks volumes concerning the hunger these men must have had for spiritual nourishment. On one such occasion, Jeff Hollenbach suggested to Bill McCartney that Jerry Gibson, one of the chaplains for the University of Illinois football team be invited to speak. He told him that Jerry visited his son quite often, and believed Jerry would be willing to speak to his group. It was not long after, that I found myself speaking at that early Morning Prayer breakfast. It was a delightful experience. My message seemed to be well-received. As I recall, I spoke to the men about *"What it means to be like Jesus,"* from the text of Romans 13: 14. However, little did I realize what a profound affect that early-morning prayer meeting was destined to have on our future ministry.

Many years passed by. One morning, shortly after moving to Colorado, I picked up "The Daily Camera" newspaper from Boulder, Colorado and turned to my number one newspaper priority, the Sports Section. There on the front page was a picture of a Bill McCartney, the Head Football Coach at the University of Colorado. I remembered the fine young coach I had met from the University of Michigan. I had fond memories of the time I met with him and the other men at the Sambo's restaurant in Ann Arbor. I wondered if he was the same man who invited me to speak to his group of men. I decided to give him a phone call. He answered the phone. I asked him if he was the same man I met at the Sambos restaurant. Upon learning it was me, he said, "Yes, I am the man. Jerry Gibson, get over here to my office beneath the football stadium right away. I want to talk with you!" Within the next hour I found myself in Bill McCartney's office, on my knees praying with that great man of God. The substance of the prayer was that God would allow the University of Colorado football team to be completely dedicated to the honor and glory of Jesus Christ. From that time on the two of us, along with others I may have brought with me, such as Danny Beaver, a former All American football player from the University of Illinois, who later became a missionary in the Philippine Islands, found ourselves on our knees on the floor of Bill McCartney's office.

God honored our prayers, and Bill McCartney's dedication. Two years later the University of Colorado won a National Championship in football!

Sal Aunese was a super talented football player for the University of Colorado football team. Out of nowhere he was diagnosed with a terminal disease. Many a prayer was offered up on his behalf. However, it was his good fortune, but for those of us he left behind, it was a time of great sorrow. I say, his good fortune, because he had accepted Jesus Christ into his heart, and was about to begin his eternal life with God in heaven. That is why, *"we sorrow not as those who have not hope,"* I Thessalonians 4: 13.

Due to the tremendous success of Colorado's football team and Sal Aunase's roll in that success, the story went national. The McCartney family immediately found themselves in the national limelight. This created many stressful situations. Fortunately, *"God's grace was sufficient for them,"* II Corinthians 12: 9.

People often ask me, "Why do bad things happen to good people like Sal Aunese's passing away in college from a terminal disease?" My reply is always the same. Bad things happen to good people if they violate either God's moral or spiritual laws. We reap what we sow, Galatians 6: 7, 8. God may be allowing our faith to be tested as in the case of Job. There is not always a simple answer. Sometimes we just do not know or understand; however, even though we may not know *what* the future holds, we can know for sure *Who* holds the future, and He promises to *"cause all things to work for the good of those who love Him and are called according to His purpose,"* Romans 8: 28. And then the most important reason of all, He may be preparing us for a very special ministry. This certainly proved to be true in the lives of Bill and Lyndi McCartney.

Not long after the passing of Sal Annessi, Dave Wardell, the former State-wide Director for the Fellowship of Christian Athletes in Colorado started to share my office at The Boulder Valley Christian Church. The two of us spent much time in sweet prayer and Christian fellowship during those days.

On one occasion, Dave Wardell accompanied Bill McCartney to a meeting in Pueblo, Colorado. On the way there and back they discussed the possibility of establishing an organization for men that seemed to have a major and minor mission. It was Bill McCartney's desire to bring together men from all denominations and diverse races and creeds and break down denominational and racial barriers in answer to Jesus' prayer for the unity of His Church, John 17. The second and lesser goal, which was championed by men such as Dave Wardell, was to remind men of the promises they made in their marriage vows — to love, honor and protect their wives and families in every manner of circumstance and be roll models. They realized that very few men were keeping the covenant they made before God and man with their wives and God. A revival was needed. Revival means, "to call back to life." They came up with the name *Promise Keepers*. When Dave Wardell met with me the next morning for prayer, he rehearsed what had taken place on the trip to Pueblo. He asked me what I thought. I told him it was an excellent idea, and worthy to pursue.

A month or so later, we made phone calls to many men in the community whom we thought might be interested in such a venture. We called for a meeting at Boulder Valley Christian Church on a Thursday evening. To my recollection, seventy men showed up! That was indeed a providential number. It recalled to my mind, *"the seventy,"* Jesus sent out as is recorded in the Tenth Chapter of Matthew. The rest is all history. Bill McCartney's dream was to possibly fill Folsom Field with men and boys. That dream was soon accomplished. Twenty-two Thousand men met at Folsom Field and eventually that led to more than a million men meeting in Washington D.C. The main goal of Promise Keepers from its inception was to answer three questions: Who are we? Where are we going? And how do we get there? The answer to these questions are: We are born again Christians; we are seeking to understand and experience God's love more; we get there through mutual worship and fellowship with men from every area of life, Galatians 3:28.

During this time I had the privilege of meeting with Bill McCartney on a regular basis as his mentor. However, I might add, he was as much, if not more of a mentor to me as I had been to him. It was a time of mutual growth for both of us. Little did we know what that humble meeting in Taylor, Michigan would lead to someday.

Bill devised a list of seven basic Christian principles as a means of measuring the spiritual growth of Christian men. He fashioned them after the game of "Twenty-one" used by basketball players. We used them together as a team. Bill would exhort on each of them and I would follow by expounding on them. As I suggested, there were seven principles. If you were still a "babe in Christ" in regard to a principle you would grade yourself with a *one*. If you were more mature but had room for growth, you gave yourself a *two*. If you believe yourself to be a mature man in Christ, you could give yourself a *three*. The highest possible score was 21. Very few men ever obtain that high a grade. In fact, Bill remarked at one time that he had never experienced anyone who claimed to be a 21. The principles are as follows:

I. Your Devotional Life. (How much time do you spend in prayer and the study of God's Word? II Timothy 2: 15; 3: 16, 17; I Thessalonians 5: 17.)

II. Your Accountability. (Is there anybody to whom you are accountable who is not afraid to ask you the tough questions-Who will confront you?)

III. Your Purity. (This mainly has to do with keeping your Holy Spirit temple pure. It has to do with sexual sins, such as pornography, I Corinthians 6: 18 ff.) If you don't turn off the picture immediately. If you watch for a while and then your conscience gets to you. You turn off the picture immediately.)

IV. Your Home Life. (This is the acid test. This is where people see you at your best as well as your worst. I Corinthians 13 is the measuring stick for this spiritual growth examination.)

V. Your Church Life. (This is what Hebrews 10: 25, 26 is all about. Do you invest your time, money and talents to further God's Kingdom?)

VI. Unity. (We are concerned more about crossing racial barriers in your Christian fellowship and outreach. Do you have racial prejudices?)

VII. Evangelism. (Are you a soul winner? Is your life an inspiration for others to want to be like Jesus? Daniel 12: 3; James 5: 20.)

This brings to mind a humorous experience. Bill and I were working together as a team for a meeting with The Fellowship of Christian Athletes at the University of Colorado. At the close of his exhortation, Bill asked, "How many of you would desire to be a 21?" With that, I stood up and expounded on the things that Bill had presented. Bill then stood up and asked, "How many of you gave yourselves a score of 21?" He asked them to stand up. Five or six young people stood up. Bill had a rather surprised look on his face. He commented that that many claiming to be a 21 had never happened before. He then asked again, "How many of the rest of you desire to attain the goal of being a 21?" He asked them to stand up. The rest of the young people stood up. After we closed with prayer, several of those who stood up claiming they were a 21 came to me and sheepishly explained they had misunderstood Bill McCartney. They thought he had asked, "How many of you are twenty one years of age?" I shared that with Bill later. We had a good chuckle over that. As I suggested earlier, Bill and I grew together in our walk with the Lord. I might add we are still growing; like the Apostle Paul, *"we have not yet arrived,"* Philippians 3: 13.

Lyndi McCartney became ill, and was unable to get away from the house without much difficulty. She was not able to breath on her own. Bill and Lyndi invited Normadeene and me, along with two other couples, Derek and Torri Fulmer and Jamie and Kristin Engelking to meet in their home for several hours on Wednesday evenings. That proved to be a time of very precious and special Christian fellowship. It was a time of accountability when we asked one another "the tough questions." It was a time when each of us measured our own spiritual growth. Each of us is still striving to be a 21. We closed our meeting with food and fellowship. We took turns bringing the deserts. The time came when it was too difficult for Lyndi to continue having guests in her home on such a regular basis. We had been praying without ceasing that God would work a healing miracle for Lyndi's physical body. However, we realize the truth and hope in the writting of the Apostle Paul when he said: *"Therefore we do not lose heart, but though our outer man is decaying, yet our inner man is being renewed day by day. For momentary light affliction is producing for us an eternal weight of glory far beyond all comparison, while we look not at the things which are seen, but at the things which are not seen; for the things which are seen are temporal, but the things which are not seen are eternal,"* II Corinthians 4: 16-18.

THE FELLOWSHIP OF CHRISTIAN FIRE FIGHTERS

Earl Justice made his influence felt in almost every area of life in Boulder. As the result, he over-extended himself. Our coming to Colorado afforded him the opportunity to shift some of his civic responsibilities to me. One of the areas was with the Boulder Fire Department. He had been serving as its Chaplain. He suggested I might be interested in taking over that area of his ministry.

As was the case with most Police Departments, very few firemen are able to cope with the crisis situations in which they find themselves where loss of life and property are involved. That is why I was made an *Honorary Chief of Police* by Chief Kelley for the City of Nashville, Tennessee. I helped train chaplains for him.

It seems a man was involved in a very serious traffic accident in which his head was cut off. The officer in charge at the Police Station called the man's wife to inform her of the tragedy. He blurted out, "Your husband was in an accident. His head was cut off." The woman suffered a heart attack and almost died. Chief Kelly reasoned there must be a better way to inform people in times of such crisis. He decided a qualified ordained minister would be ideal for the task. They were experienced in bringing comfort and solace at such times. He was right.

The same is true with Firemen. I had this vividly brought to my attention shortly after I took over the position as Chaplain for the Boulder Fire Department. Soon after I was introduced to Chief Boyce, Boulder's Fire Chief, and was approved and installed as the new Chaplain, I received a call early one morning, informing me of an apartment house complex fire. I was on twenty-four hour call and had been given a radio-controlled monitoring device that kept me informed of any action in which the Fire Department was involved. I was also issued a picture ID that gave me the authority to be in places off limits to the general public. I might add, at first, many police officers, firemen, as well as other city officials, never fully accepted my position as being necessary. Fortunately, many of them changed their opinion after getting to know me and observe my actions in times of crisis. I jumped into my car and drove rapidly to the scene of the fire. One of the apartments was enveloped in a raging inferno. Chief Boyce approached me and informed me that they believed that at least one person was trapped in his or her apartment. An attempted rescue operation was in progress. He told me a Command Post had been set up in one of the apartments far enough away from the fire to be safe. He said the people who were successfully evacuated were there and needed me for comfort and encouragement. He said many of them would lose most of their earthly possessions and some were in danger of losing family members as well as close friends. Tables had been set up containing coffee and other refreshments. There were several nurses as well social workers present, also.

Word came that the rescuers had recovered the charred remains of a man, and I believe, a small child in the smoldering ashes of one of the apartments. I heard a loud cry followed by a terrifying scream! It came from the wife and mother of the victims who had been identified. I rushed to her side, took her hand, and prayed for her. The bodies had not yet been positively identified, so I suggested in my prayer, perhaps they were not her husband and child. Her loud wailing turned to sobs, but sobs of anguish, because she had already accepted the worst. Unfortunately, she was right. She thanked me for being there for her at a time when she needed me the most. However, I was rebuked by several police officers for praying with her before they were positively identified. I have often said, "The same sun that melts wax, hardens clay."

I leaned later that Cliff Mealy lived in one of the apartment complexes that was badly damaged by smoke and water.

I was convinced the office of Chaplain for the Fire Department was needed. I made it a point to visit each of the many Fire Stations in the Boulder area at least once a week. I found it to be very time-consuming. I was received by most of them with open arms. It was during one of those visits that I became very close to a husband and wife team, Bryan and Sarah Ruff. They started attending the Boulder Valley Christian Church where I was, at that time, the Interim Minister. They had a beautiful daughter with whom we soon fell in love. Bryan and Sarah entertained us in their home often. They asked me to teach them about *the design and purpose of Christian baptism.* As the result, I had the privilege of baptizing them into Christ.

Some time later, while we were traveling, Bryan suffered a fatal heart attack. By that time, Dave Roadcup had taken on the duty of Senior Minister for the Boulder Valley Christian Church, and was there for Sarah in her time of great sorrow. We returned home just in time for Bryan's funeral. The church was packed with fellow firemen, policemen, government officials, as well as friends and relatives. Dave Roadcup's message offered comfort and hope to all who were present.

At about this time, we learned of an organization known as The Fellowship of Christian Fire Fighters. Sam Donges, a Volunteer Fireman from the Boulder Valley Christian Church, was a member of the organization. Through his influence, I became a member. The organization was intended to help fire fighters deal with the emotions they encountered during crisis situations. At the time, I thought the organization was much needed. However, after attending a

Fellowship of Christian Fire Fighters Convention in Steamboat Springs, I decided it was not fulfilling its intended mission and purpose.

After I was a member about two years, Chief Boyce, who had become one of my very close friends decided to retire. Things were never the same. The new Fire Chief saw little need for a Chaplain. I just faded away. However, I kept in contact with many whose friendship remains to this day.

THE FELLOWSHIP OF CHRISTIAN ATHLETES

While we were with the University of Illinois, with the help of Coach Harve Schmidt, Don Kessenger, from the Chicago Cubs, and Jeff Hollenbach, Quarterback for the University or Illinois, we were instrumental in establishing a Chapter of Fellowship of Christian Athletes. This proved to be a strong influence in the direction of our ministry for years to come. We worked with the Fellowship of Christian Athletes at Northern Mississippi University while we were with Mid-South Christian College. And one of the first things we did, upon arriving in Colorado, was to establish a relationship with the University of Colorado's FCA It was there that we became close friends of Coach Dan Stavely and Dave Wardell, who at that time was the State Director of the FCA.

The first meetings we attended were conducted under the Bleachers at Colorado's football field, Folsom Stadium. Soon after attending that first meeting, I was asked to teach a Bible class for the adult sponsors. As I recall, it was there that we met Wendell and "Gabby," Barbara Burchett. We have been close friends ever since.

Men and women athletes from every athletic program were actively involved in FCA We started our mentoring program at the university with these athletes. The FCA meetings were conducted at first in the University Field House. Later they were held in the Dow Ward Athletic Center.

The meetings began with a lively, well-organized, song service. Prayers and personal testimonies of how Christ had influenced the lives of the athletes followed the singing. That was followed by an inspirational speaker. I was asked to speak on several occasions. And those opportunities proved to be the exposure I needed that caused athletes to ask me to mentor them.

This began a steady stream of young men and women desiring to be baptized into Christ. Most of them came to the university possessing the faith they had received from their mothers and fathers. However, they did not have a faith of their own. As suggested often, God has no grandchildren. It was a thrill to see the change in the lives of these Christian Athletes after they found a faith of their own.

Some of the young men had been sleeping with their girlfriends, and some of the young women had been sleeping with their boyfriends. That was the accepted norm on the campus. After they *buried the old dead man,* and *put on their Jesus suits.* Romans 6: 1-5; Galatians 3: 27, they did not have sex until after they were married. This proved to be a tremendous testimony for the rest of the athletes.

THE DESIGN AND PURPOSE OF CHRISTIAN BAPTISM

I recently received a letter from a former student at the University of Illinois. It was a pleasant surprise, as I had not heard from her for many years. She was one of the young college students we baptized while we were ministering there on the university campus and the Webber Street Christian Church. Her name is Ann Ruppe Farrington. She shared with me some important things that had happened to her since we last saw her. She concluded her letter by saying, "I have gone back to the Webber Street Christian Church. That's my home. I bet you remember all the college kids and younger kids you baptized. The mid-1970's was a great time."

She was right. I have fond memories of the young men and women I had the privilege of baptizing back in the mid-1970s. However, since then I have had the privilege of baptizing many more. That is especially true in the seventeen years we have spent as campus ministers at the University of Colorado.

As I contemplate the joyous experience of baptizing so many college age young people, I cannot help but wonder why they have been so open to the simple teachings of the Bible in regard to this very important subject. I say, "important" because it is one of the two ordinances Jesus gave us in the New Testament. The Lord's Supper is the other. Both of them proclaim the fact of Jesus' death for our sins, burial, and resurrection from the dead. I Corinthians 11: 23-26; Romans 6: 1-5. The Christian Church has been divided over the design and purpose of Christian baptism since the church was first established. I believe that is the result of an authority crisis. We should ask ourselves, "Where do we get our authority for the things we teach as necessary as a *test of fellowship* in our churches?" The problem we face is a matter of "authority."

While we were in China, and later on in Korea, we saw the problem vividly. The Fellowship of Christian Servicemen had as its theme, "One in Christ." It was very frustrating for many that attended, because many of them did not have the Bible as their basis of authority. Whenever we had the opportunity, we urged the Korean Christians to read what Historians, who lived in Jesus' day had to say about Him, and to give their testimony as to how *He* had touched their lives.

A BITTERSWEET REVELATION

After about our fourth week in Colorado, a very disturbing thing took place. As a result, Earl Justice, the Senior Minister of the Boulder Valley Christian Church, who was instrumental in getting us to Colorado, was forced to resign due to some very serious personal problems. We were sure we would be asked to leave due to our close ties with Earl. However, that was not the case. The elders approached me and requested me to serve as the interim minister for the Boulder Valley Christian Church, as they would need time for healing and also to secure a permanent Senior Minister. God indeed can take our bad times and turn them into good times. As Normadeene and I look back we realize there was no way we could have survived financially had the circumstances been different. They agreed to pay us a salary equal to whatever we needed until were able to raise a financial base for our mission. They also agreed to serve as a covering for our mission until we were able to obtain 50l-(C) 3 Not-for-Profit Incorporation status for World-Wide Missions Outreach. God certainly takes care of fools, and Jerry and Normadeene Gibson too.

OUR FIRST BIG CHALLENGE

It was Tuesday evening. Several members of the choir were practicing for an upcoming program. One of the young ladies present, who was very active in the music program of the church, seemed to be pre-occupied. I inquired as to what was troubling her. She told me she had a quarrel with her husband before leaving for the church. They were currently babysitting for a young couple that was on a cruise. The husband was not happy about being left alone at home with the baby boy.

Shortly after I arrived back home, my telephone rang. It was Doug Chastain, one of the Associate Ministers of the church. He said an emergency had arisen and asked me to accompany him to the hospital. The little boy that the church member was babysitting had stopped breathing and was rushed to a nearby hospital.

As I look back in retrospect, after eighteen years, I realize more now than ever, the significance of the things that transpired that night. Doug and I found ourselves in the lobby of a nearby hospital, only to be told that the little boy had been taken in critical condition from there by a flight to life helicopter to Children's hospital in Denver. We were about to spend one of the longest nights of our lives.

The baby's mother and father were on their way home from their vacation. We were told that they had been notified their baby boy was in Children's Hospital. No details were given to them at that time, other than that there had been a terrible accident and they should come to the hospital as soon as possible. It was going to be my lot to fill them in with the details of which, at the time, I had no knowledge other than that their baby boy was in intensive care. Upon inquiring, I learned that the distraught husband told the authorities that the baby had fallen out of his crib and injured his head. Upon further inquiry he changed his story and said that the baby was crying and in an attempt to quiet him, he gently shook the baby. He never admitted to shaking the little boy in an abusive manner, however.

My heart sunk within me when we entered the room and saw the lifeless body of that beautiful little boy lying there in a crib. I wondered how I could inform his mother and father. What could I say to comfort them and give them some hope? I thought of many scriptures, but at the time, none of them seemed adequate. We bowed our heads and prayed for wisdom.

That's all one can do at a time like that. In the words of Peter to Jesus when Jesus asked him after Jesus had fed the multitudes who left Him after their stomachs were full, if he and the other disciples would leave him too, *"Lord to whom would we go, for you have the words of life,"* John 6: 68. I remembered the words of David after his son had died, *"You can't come to me, but I can come to you,"* II Samuel 12: 23. We hoped it would not go that far; we contemplated the worst that could happen.

I wondered why the babysitting husband was not there at the hospital with us. Of all people, he should have been the one with the deepest concern. Several hours passed by, and he still was not there.

I was sitting in a waiting room, and saw him come into the room. I jumped up to greet him with an assuring hug. It was then that I knew something was very wrong. He reeked with the smell of alcohol! I immediately wondered if while under the influence, he lost his patience, along with his temper, with the little boy's crying and literally shook the baby to death. I also wondered why I was the only one to notice he had been drinking. It seemed like everybody was trying to protect him, rather than feel sympathy for the mother and father and the little boy who never came out of the coma.

I continued to ponder what words of comfort I could give to the little boy's mother and father. I prayed without ceasing that the boy would come out of the coma and survive the shaking trauma. Imagine what it would be like to place your baby in the care of trusted friends or neighbors, and come home to a situation like this! Child abuse is becoming more and more a problem in this day and age. We must provide ways to protect innocent children! We must ask if there are some warning signals that may alert us and make possible our preventing such a tragedy from happening.

The time I dreaded was upon me. A young couple came into the hospital lobby. I immediately thought, "they must be the little boy's parents." One could tell by the looks of desperation on their faces that it was their little boy who was fighting for his life. I followed them into the room where their little boy was lying in a crib. His mother began to scream and sob the words, "No! No! No! Why God? Why God? Why God? Why our little boy?" I put my arms around her and the baby's father and plead with God to provide comfort for them, something only He could supply for a situation and time like that. I prayed the words of Psalms 46, *"God is our refuge and strength, a very present help in trouble. Therefore we will not fear." "Be still and know that I am God,"* and also Jesus' words in John 14: 1 *"Let not your hearts be troubled, you believe in God, believe also in me . . ."* A feeling of peace permeated the room. It was as though God was hugging the weeping mother and father. Yes, whom could we go to besides Jesus at a time such as this?

Not long after, the little baby boy was pronounced dead. I tried to console his mother and father, but nothing anyone could do or say seemed to be able to heal the hurt they were feeling. I wondered how the young man who had been left in charge of their little boy could face them. What could he say or do? Nothing he could say or do could ever bring their baby back to them. Like David of old, *"He could not come to them, but some day they would be able to go to him,"* II Samuel 12: 23.

The babysitter was arrested on charges of manslaughter. This led to a lengthy as well as heartbreaking trial. Many of his friends came to his defense with character references, but I suspected all of the time that he was guilty, and would have to pay for his crime. Even after that, he would have to live with himself. If you pound a nail in the wood and then pull it out, the nail is gone, but the scar is still there.

The young man served several years in prison. While he was there, his wife divorced him, and then married one of his friends. Yes, when we sin, like David, we may not take the entire nation into it with us; however, you can be sure we will take the ones we love the most into it with us. Psalms 51 depicts the plaintiff cry of David as he pleads with God, *"Take not thy Holy Spirit from me!"* He saw what happened with Saul and did not want to suffer the same woeful fate. I am sure that young man prayed that same prayer over and over again. The sad thing was that nothing could be done to bring that little boy back to his parents.

I have often commented on the many privileges afforded ministers of the Gospel. Even though situations like the one I just shared with you are very difficult to handle, they cannot begin to compare with the many areas of blessing afforded Christian ministers. We have the privilege of officiating at marriage ceremonies. We are the first to be called on for prayer when a loved one is taken to the hospital due to critical illness. We have the privilege of helping new parents dedicate themselves to raising their children in a Christian home. We bury people in baptism and help them begin their journey as a Christians. We conduct the memorial service for loved ones as they begin their birthday in heaven. All things being equal, nobody gains more respect in the community than the Christian minister. Yes, we may well ask ourselves in the words that Satan questioned Job's faithfulness to God, *"Do we fear God for naught?"* Job 1: 9.

CHRISTIAN STUDENT FELLOWSHIP BOOTH AT THE UMC

The University of Colorado campus is very beautiful. It took us a long time getting used to seeing the Flatirons Mountains, a natural background for the campus, and farther behind, the majestic front range of the Rocky Mountains. It was, and still is, an awe inspiring, breath taking experience. As we drove from Lafayette to the university each morning we were tempted to pinch ourselves to see if we actually live here and if we are actually experiencing it with our own eyes.

As I write this chapter, we have completed nineteen wonderful years of ministry at the University of Colorado. I still remember the feeling of excitement I experienced as I parked my car in front of the CU Memorial Center (UMC) and walked up the brick stairs into the building. To my right, as I entered was the Glen Miller Ballroom. To the left was the receptionist desk. Donna Hogstrom was the receptionist. We became very close friends after our first meeting. I inquired of her as to the location of the Students Services Office. She directed me to an elevator that took me to the second floor where the Student Services offices were located.

As I entered the office, I was greeted warmly by a young lady. She turned out to be the coordinator of Student Services. I informed her as to who I was and what my mission was at the university. John Morphue had registered the campus ministry sponsored by Boulder Valley Christian Church under the name Christian Student Fellowship. It is important to have authorized recognized university status in order to have access to the university facilities.

I filled out some papers and paid a twenty-five dollar activity fee, and was now a registered campus minister.

I was told I had two options as to how I conducted my ministry on the campus. I could either have a small office on the second floor of the Memorial Center, or have a table, which they referred to as a booth, on the ground floor next to the cafeteria. I opted for the booth next to the cafeteria. The way to a man's heart is still through his stomach.

I prepared a large sign with the words: Christian Student Fellowship, followed by the statement: "Everything you ever wanted to know about the Bible." That was followed by the question: "How well do you know your Bible?" And then came an invitation to take a Bible aptitude test I had prepared. They were a series of true or false questions, taken form both the Old and New Testaments, which were an excellent gage of one's overall knowledge of the Bible. That proved to be very valuable, as it led to many of the teaching opportunities that have been afforded me through the past eighteen years in the university community. The following is the examination I gave to answer the question, how well do you know your Bible?

A recent study reveals that 75 to 80 percent of those, who claim to be Christian, never study their Bible at all. Many people know "about" the Bible, but do not "know" the Bible. Below you will fine a list of questions taken from both the Old and New testaments that will measure your Basic Bible aptitude. If you are not satisfied with your knowledge of the Bible, we will provide special Bible classes to meet your particular interests and needs.

The classes will be taught by Dr. Jerry Gibson, a former president of Mid-South Christian College, and professor at Minnesota Bible College in Minneapolis, Minnesota and the University of Illinois. Please avail yourself of this excellent opportunity to really "know" your Bible.

BIBLE QUIZ

(Circle True or False):

1. T F God "Created" three things as recorded in Genesis 1.

2. T F The Bible records that both man and woman were made in God's image.

3. T F Adam was not present when Eve was tempted.

4. T F The precedent for the father giving away the bride is set by God in the Bible.

5. T F Adam was "molded" from the dust of the earth.

6. T F The Bible records that animals are "living souls."

7. T F The Bible teaches that there was "light" before there was a sun.

8. T F Man and woman were both created as "responsible beings."

9. T F The rivers Pizon, Tigris, Euphrates, and Indus were all in the Garden

10. T F Men began to call upon the name of the Lord during the time of Seth.

11. T F Noah and his family were the only humans who survived the flood.

12. T F The longest life span recorded after the flood was shorter than the shortest before the flood.

13. T F Enoch was the only man in the Bible who did not die a physical death.

14. T F All of the major races today stem from Noah's three sons

15. T F Noah was the first recorded "drunk man" in the Bible

16. T F Shem sinned and was cursed by Noah.

17. T F Jewish History begins with Abraham's call in Genesis 12.

18. T F Jewish History begins with the Exodus.

19. T F   Sarah is the only woman whose age is recorded in the Bible.

20. T F   Sarah was Abraham's sister.

21. T F   Matthew is one of the Synoptic Gospels.

22. T F   Luke records Jesus' genealogy from the time of Adam.

23. T F   Moses appears with Jesus in the Book of Matthew.

24. T F   The New Testament speaks of five different baptisms.

25. T F   Love is considered in I Corinthians as greater than spiritual gifts.

These questions served as an excellent motivator for university students being a part of a Bible study group.

Not long after I started working at the CU Memorial Center, I was invited to Colorado State University by a group of university professors and friends of Doug and Beth Keasling. They had heard about my booth and wanted to know the most often asked questions by students and faculty members. It proved to be a very interesting and rewarding experience, as it opened the door for many future meetings with members of the group. The following is what shared with them, and continue to share with others until this day.

QUESTIONS MOST OFTEN ASKED AT THE UMC BOOTH

II Timothy 2: 2; 2: 15; 3: 16, 17.

Introduction: The questions fall mainly into three major categories:

1. Theological: Define Theology –The Bible plus human Philosophy.
2. Moral and Ethical: Are there divine absolutes? What does the Bible say? The Ten Commandments. What do the New Testament writers say?
3. Philosophical: Man's wisdom apart from the Bible. Existentialism, etc.

MOST OFTEN ASKED QUESTIONS

1. How can we know the Bible is really God's Word; and why is it superior to the Book of Mormon, etc? The following scriptures should be considered: II Timothy 3:16,17 Galatians 1: 11; II Peter 1: 18-21; Isaiah 40: 8.

2. Why don't we have the Apocryphal Books in our Bible when they are in the Roman Catholic Bible? (They bridge the gap between the Old and New Testaments and Provide some valuable history. However they do not rise to the status of being canonical.)

3. Why does a just, loving God allow evil and suffering? Why do bad things happen to good people? (This is the theme of the Book of Job — why do the righteous suffer?)

    A. Bad things happen to good people for four basic reasons:

    1. When we violate either God's physical, moral or spiritual laws. We reap what we sow. Galatians 6: 7, 8.

    2. As in the case of the Book of Job, God may be allowing our faith to be tested. The Satan questions Job's motives. He accused Job of fearing God for purely selfish reasons. We would do well to examine our own motives.

    3. We don't know why bad things happen to good people in many instances. However, we do know that God specializes in taking our bad times and turning them into good times. Romans 8: 28 and I Corinthians 10: 13 assure this to be true.

    4. God may be preparing us for a very special ministry. We have to have our hearts broken a few times before we can really be a power for God. The ones we love the most are often the first ones to break our hearts. We can not say we understand someone's suffering unless we have experienced the same kind suffering ourselves.

4. Would a loving God send a person to hell? God emptied heaven in order to make possible salvation for everybody. We choose for ourselves where we will spend eternity. The following scriptures should be considered: John 3: 16; Matthew 18: 14; II Peter 3: 9; John 10: 28, 29; John 12: 48; I Timothy 2: 4.

5. Is there really a Devil? I John 3: 8 says there is.

6. Is there a heaven and a hell? The following are scriptures to be considered: Mark 9: 47; Luke 16: 23, Revelation 20: 19; Revelation 21: 8. Three Greek words should be considered when discussing the topic of hell: Gehenna, Tartaroos; and Hades. They must be understood in the light of the context in which they are found. The Hebrew "sheol" is translated "hell" or "the grave." It simply refers to "the abode of the dead."

7. Is baptism essential to salvation? Define Salvation." Greek, "Soterion." Luke 7:30; Mark l6: 16; Acts 2: 38: Acts 22: 16; Galatians 3: 27; I Peter 3: 21.

8. How can I know God's will for my life? Colossians 3: 17; I John 2: 1-18.

9. Why are there so many different denominations of churches? John 17:20; I Corinthians 2:3.

10. Is it wrong to have sex before marriage? I Corinthians 6: 9, 10; & I Corinthians 6: 18ff.

11. What about Abortion? Does a woman have the right to choose? Psalms 139: 13; Exodus-20: 13.

12. Is homosexuality really a sin? I Corinthians 6: 9, Leviticus 18: 22, 20: 13. If people do not desire this life style, they can change: The following are necessary to help bring about the change in life style: Recognize how I became a homosexual-Most likely the result of "Same sex ambivalence." Recognize it is a process. Establish healthy same sex relationships. Can only be successful with the help of the Holy Spirit, which we receive when one becomes a Christian.

13. Where was God when my friend was killed? God has not moved. He was the same place he was when Jesus died on the cross.

14. What is the roll of women in the Church? What about women ministers, elders, teachers, Galatians 3:28; I Peter 3:1-8; I Corinthians 11: 1-3; I Corinthians 14: 34; I Timothy 2: 9-15.

15. Are charismatic gifts for today? Acts 8:18; I Corinthians 12 :31;

16. Are the Ten Commandments for today? Colossians 2:14; Matthew 22: 33ff.

17. Why did a moral God demand the destruction of the Caananites? Isaiah 1:4-6

18. What about divorce? Is it ever right for a Christian to get a divorce? I Corinthians 7: 1ff. Mark 10: 1-12.

19. What about Capitol Punishment? Romans 13.

20. Is it wrong to kill in war, or even to go to war? Romans 14: 23.

Normadeene and I have spent most of our lives on university campuses answering questions such as these, as well as many others that trouble the minds of our world's young people in this age at the end of an age in which we live.

A law professor gave a different exam to his students at the close of each semester. On one such occasion, he handed the exam questions to his secretary. She glanced at the questions and then exclaimed, "Professor, these are the same questions you gave to the last semester class!" He quickly replied, "That's right. The questions are the same, but the answers are different." We would do well to think about what the professor said. Perhaps we need to come up with some different and better answers that will satisfy the needs of our college age young people.

Albus Brooks was the name of the young football player. I mentored him several years while he was attending the University of Colorado. He is now the Director of The Denver District for Young Life, and is having a very successful ministry. I received a phone call from one of the young University of Colorado football players asking for scriptures to memorize that he could use as a special resource. He wanted passages of scripture that he could quote when being tempted to do things he knew were not good for him or his Christian walk. He called me all of the way from Hawai'i where the university was playing in a bowl game. I often point out to those I mentor the best way to overcome temptation is to say, "In the name of Jesus get behind me Satan," and then quote a Bible verse that specifically pertains to the issue you are facing.

I embarrassed Normadeene one time when we were confronted by a group of New Age false prophets. We were about to enter a department store in Champaign, Illinois. They were handing out tracts that contained their false teachings. I said to them, "In the name of Jesus get thee behind me Satan," and quoted Galatians 1: 8, 9, "*Though we or an angel from heaven should preach to you a gospel contrary to that which we have preached to you, let him be accursed. As we have said before, if any man is preaching to you* contrary *to that which you received, let him be accursed.*" They immediately ran away from us.

I intended to list only a few scriptures from both the Old and New Testaments. However I ended up with a rather lengthy list of Bible verses; each one of these is a passage I often use as a resource when I am counseling people that are facing difficult situations in their lives. The list is as follows:

THE QUICK AND THE POWERFUL
Hebrews 4:12 &13; II Timothy 3:16, l, II Timothy 2:2 & 2:15
(From the Old Testament)

A verse for all seasons
(We *must* be able to give a reason for what we believe to those who ask)
I Peter 3:15

1. Genesis 3:15	27. Psalms 51:1-17	53. Ezekiel 3:5
2. Genesis 12:1-3	28. Psalms 91: 16	54. Ezekiel 18:8
3. Genesis 15:6	29. Psalms 103: 1-22	55. Ezekiel 33:11
4. Genesis 18:19 & 25	30. Psalms 107:23-31	56. Hosea 4:6
5. Genesis 22:12	31. Psalms 118:8,9	57. Joel 3:9-17
6. Genesis 31:49	32. Psalms 119:11 &105	58. Amos 4:12
7. Exodus 20:3-17.	33. Psalms 127:1	59. Micah 5:2 & 6:8
8. Leviticus 19:18	34. Psalms 139:1-23	60. Hab. 1:5
9. Deuteronomy 6: 3-9	35. Psalms 150:1-6	61. Hab. 2:4
10. Joshua 1:7	36. Proverbs 3:5,6	62. Zech. 4:6

11. Joshua 14:12.

12. Joshua 24:15

13. Judges 16:22

14. Ruth 1:16

15. I Samuel 12:22-24

16. I Samuel 5:22

17. I Samuel 16:7

18. I Samuel 24:14.

19. II Chronicles 7:14

20. Psalms 1:1-3

21. Psalms 14:1 & 53:1

22. Psalms 16:9,10

23. Psalms 22: 1-18

37. Proverbs 6:16-19 & 27 &28

38. Proverbs 14:12

39. Proverbs 29:18

40. Job 19: 25,26

41. Ecclesiastes 12:1,&2 & 13&14

42. Song of Solomon 8:6

43. Isaiah 7:14 , 30:15

44. Isaiah 45:8

45. Isaiah 53:1-12

46. Isaiah 54:1,2

47. Isaiah 55:1-3

48. Isaiah 61:1-3

49 Isaiah 65:24

63. Malachi 3:10

64. Malachi 4:5

65. Daniel 1:8

66. Daniel 3:17,18

67. Psalms 23

68. Psalms 46:1-11

69. Jeremiah 6:16

70. Jer.7:31; 20:9

71. Jer. 20:9,10

72. Jer. 32:35

73. Lam. 3:22-25

THE QUICK AND POWERFUL
(From the New Testament)

1. Matthew 1:23

2. Matthew 3:13-17

3. Matthew 6:33

4. Mathew 10:32,33

5. Matthew 16:13-19

6. Matthew 17:1-5

7. Matthew 18:

8. Matthew 25:31-46

9. Matthew 26:26-28

10. Matthew 28:18-20

26. John 11:25,26

27. John 12:48

28. John 13:17;23-26;34,35

29. John 14:1-6;15

30. John 15:5

31. John 17: 20;26

32. John 20: 30,31

33. John 22:23

34. Acts 1:8, 21,22

35. Acts 2: 36-47

51. Romans 10:9,10;17

52. Romans 16:17

53. I Cor. 1:18;21

54. I Cor. 2:1,2; 13-16

55. I Cor. 3:1-3; 11

56. I Cor. 7:1-5

57. I Cor. 8:9-13

58. I Cor. 10:1-1

59. I Cor. 12:12-14

60. I Cor. 13: 1-13

76. Col. 2:12

77. Col. 3: 1-14

78. I Thes.4:13-18

79. I Thes. 5:17, 18

80. I Tim. 1:9,10

81. I Tim.3:1-10

82. I Tim. 5:1

83. I Tim. 6:10

84. II Tim. 1:6,7

85. II Tim.2:2;15

11. Mark 3:22-30	36. Acts 5:32	61. I Cor. 14:33	86. II Tim. 3:16,17
12. Mark 10:13-15	37. Acts 6:4	62. I Cor. 15:1-4; 50-58	87. II Tim. 4:1-8
13. Mark 13:10	38. Acts 8:12; 18; 26-40	63. II Cor. 4:7-17	88. Titus 3:5
14. Mark 15:15,16	39. Acts 10: 34; 47,48	64. II Cor. 9:6-8	89. Heb. 5:11-14
15. Luke 7:30	40. Acts 13:1-3	65. Gal. 1:8,9	90. Heb 6:4-6
16. Luke 15:7	41. Acts 16:30	66. Gal. 3:27-29	91. Heb. 9:16
17. Luke 16:31	42. Acts 17:30	67. Gal. 5:4; 16-26	92. Heb. 10:25,26
18. Luke 19:10	43. Acts 18:8	68. Gal. 6:1-3; 7-14	93. Heb. 11:1-6
19. Luke 24:44-49	44. Acts 19:1-6	69. Eph. 1:3; 18-23	94. James 1:5
20. John 1:1-5	45. Acts 20:7; 26-35	70. Eph. 4:14-22	95. James 2:26
21. John 3:1-5	46. Acts 22:16	71. Eph. 5:21-33	96. James 5:14-20
22. John 4:24	47. Romans 1:16	72. Eph. 6: 10-18	97. I Pet 3:21
23. John 6:35	48. Romans 5:1-8	73. Philip. 1:21, 2:5ff.	98. II Pet. 1:3
24. John 7:38	49. Romans 6:1-5; 16-18	74. Philip. 4:4-13	99. I John 1:6-10
25. John 8:7	50. Romans 8: 18-39	75. Col. 1:18	100. Rev. 22:18ff

INTERNATIONAL STUDENTS
(Our prophetic logo-Mu Jie Lin and Shaddrack Kemenya)

Our Logo, "From Boulder, Colorado to Beijing, China, proved to be prophetic. Soon after we arrived in Colorado, a very dear friend, Suan Schnell introduced us to the Economic Institute on the University of Colorado campus. It housed the largest number of International students in any one place in America. We agreed to be a part of its Host Family program that provided a home away from home for Internationals. We suggested we preferred to host either African or Chinese students. Soon after, we received the papers of Mu Jie Lin, a Chinese International student from Beijing, China. It was love at first sight. Mu Jie Lin soon became a part of our family. Even though he was a Chinese Communist, he attended services regularly at the Boulder Valley Christian Church, and accompanied me to a Men's Retreat at Camp Como, near Fairplay, Colorado. He enjoyed his time at Camp Como, expressing to me that it was the most enjoyable experience he had ever had in his life.

Mu Jie Lin was an interpreter for the Chinese government. He was attending the Economic Institute to improve his communications skills with business men. He asked Normadeene and me to help in with the English language. We agreed to do so and asked him if it was alright for us to use the Bible as our text. He agreed to that and promptly invited several other Chinese men and women to meet with us. We became very close friends to many of them.

I decided to use the New Testament Gospel of John as our text for teaching them English. I was convinced that the Holy Spirit, working through God's word, would convince them that Jesus was the Son of God. Our group grew from four to eight people in a short time, John 20: 30, 31.

The Chinese people are not very demonstrative so one can seldom know what they are thinking. One day we were discussing John 14: 6, where Jesus says, "I am the way, the truth and the life, and no one comes unto the Father, except by me." Somehow, that struck a tone. With one accord they began to shout, "We believe! We believe! We believe!" Not long after, most of them were baptized into Christ.

JERRY'S GEMS — STANDLEY LAKE HIGH SCHOOL

A group of high school administrators, teachers and coaches met with me every Wednesday morning at 6:00 a.m. at the Standley Lake High School for seven years for a Bible Study. When I decided to no longer continue meeting with the group, they asked me to put together some of the sayings that I often used while leading their Bible Study. The following is a representative example of what they called "Jerry's Gems."

As a member of the group of people classified as "Senior Citizens," these are the kind of things I use when I disciple young and old people alike. The words of Ecclesiastes l2: l is what I believe should be the motivation for all Christians who have reached the evening of life in their Christian walk. *"Remember thy Creator in the in the days of thy youth . . . ."* Why is this so important? So that we do not do things when we are young that we will be sorry for all of the rest of our lives!

God has given us the freedom to make choices, but has not given us the freedom to choose the consequences. Every choice has its consequences. We reap what we sow. Gal. 6: 7, 8. The devil blinds us to everything but the immediate pleasure of sin. But he doesn't let us see the future consequences. In other words, the devil can get you into hell, but cannot get you out! That is why Proverbs l4: l2 warns, *"There is a way that seems right unto a man, but the end thereof is the way of death."*

As older, mature Christians, we should be role models and mentors to those who come after us. We should strive to reach our full potential in every area of the Christian life. People become like what they see. We should strive to reach the place in our lives that we can say what the great Apostle Paul said to the Corinthian Church. *"Be ye followers of me, as I also am of Christ,"* I Corinthians 11: 1.

The following collection of my favorite phrases is not in any particular order, but was written just as they were recalled to mind.

Jerry's Gems

1. God will stay by your side, if you stay by His side. He has not moved.

2. It is possible to give without loving, but it is impossible to love without giving, John 3:16.

3. Cursed be the man who first said, "It's mine."

4. Sin is a monster of such frightful mean, that to be hated, needs only to be seen. But seen too often familiar with its face, first we abhor, then we endure, and then we embrace.

5. The devil can get you into hell, but he cannot get you out.

6. The devil blinds us to everything but the immediate pleasure of sin. He doesn't let us see the future consequences.

7. God has given us the freedom to make choices, but He has not given us the freedom to choose the consequences. Every choice has its consequences. We are reaping a harvest from making bad choices.

8. It's not what you say that hurts you, but what some fool said you said.

9. Josh Billings said, "It ain't what you don't know that hurts you, but what you do know that ain't so!"

10. God intended for people to be loved and things to be used. We have reversed the order. We love things and use people.

11. Love is a funny thing shaped like a lizard. It climbs down your throat and grabs at your gizzard!

12. Spiritual maturity is not in knowing what we want and how to get it. It is in knowing what we possess and how to give it, Acts 20:35.

13. Fair weather Christians are a dime a dozen.

14. You cannot have the Lord's Supper and the devil's desert!

15. When you speak: stand up, speak up and shut up.

16. In regard to a boring speech, in the oil business, if we have not struck oil in a reasonable length of time, we stop boring.

17. People go to church Lord's Day after Lord's Day, expecting to hear nothing, and they are seldom disappointed.

18. Almighty dollar, thy shiny face bespeaks thy wondrous power. Come dwell within my pocket here. I need thee every hour. The Miser's prayer.

19. To fail to plan is to plan to fail.

20. Beauty is only skin deep. Ugliness goes all of the way to the bone.

21. Dear Lord, make the words that I speak today tender, because I may have to eat them tomorrow.

22. We may not know what the future holds, but we can be sure as to who holds the future.

23. We can do what we know we cannot do, with the help of God.

24. We should work as though all depends upon us. And we should pray as though all depends upon God.

25. Jesus was not sent He went.

26. Where was God when my friend was killed? He was the same place He was when Jesus died on the cross. He has not moved.

27. How big was the cross? It was big enough to hold the sins of the world for all eternity!

28. It's hard to be humble when you're great. However, the truth is humble.

29. The best test of a man's character is a golf ball in the rough with nobody looking but God.

30. The only shot that's important is the next shot. Walter Hagen

31. The past is not to be lived in but learned by.

32. Impression without expression, leads to depression.

33. If you can keep your composure, when all around you are losing theirs, chances are, you Don't understand the situation!

34. The holiest place to be when you are sick, or tired, is in bed.

35. The safest place to be, is where God wants you to be.

36. Three words that are key to success: work, work, work!

37. A person's intelligence is in direct proportion to his or her ability to adjust themselves to the situation at hand.

38. Man proposes, but it is God who disposes!

39. God's time is the best time.

40. Jesus never hurried, never worried, and He never doubted the outcome.

41. More can be accomplished in a short time when people are ready, than in a long time when they are not ready.

42. God can take our bad times and turn them into good times.

43. Change a man against his will, he is of the same opinion still.

44. Start with people where you find them, not where you want them to be.

45. It is not the short run, but the long haul that counts.

46. If you ever find a perfect church, don't join it, because you will ruin it.

47. Make people think they think, and they will love you. Make people think, and they will hate you.

48. Five percent of the people think. Fifteen percent think they think. Eighty percent would rather die than think!

49. Too many people place a question mark where God has placed a period. They accept God's facts, but draw their own conclusions.

50. The more logical a theory may seem, the more erroneous it may be, if it is based on a faulty major premise.

51. The conscience is not an informer, it is an accuser. The intellect informs, the conscience accuses. Therefore, if your thinking is wrong, your conscience will also be wrong!

52. Toss a rock into a pack of hounds and the one that howls is the one you hit.

53. The world will never be WON for Christ, until those of us who claim to be Christians are ONE, John 17.

54. The essence of a circle is not in its bigness, but in its roundness.

55. *J E S U S:* *J*ust *E*xactly *S*uits *U*s *S*inners!

56. The only difference in the words *UNITED* and *UNTIED* is the position of the *I* !

57. Christ alone can save the world, but Christ cannot save the world alone. John 20: 21

58. When the going gets tough, the tough get going!

59. You can't teach an old dog new tricks. You can't teach a lazy dog new tricks. We must never stop learning.

60. You may not be able to keep a bird from flying over your head. However, you can keep it from building a nest in your hair!

61. You take care of your character and leave your reputation up to God.

62. Wrong is still wrong if everybody is doing it. Right is still right, if nobody is doing it!

63. God and one man is always a majority!

64. It is alright for a ship to be in the ocean, but it is not alright for the ocean to be in the ship. It is alright for the church to be in the world, but it is not alright for the world to be in the church, I John 2: 15-17.

65. The only thing that we learn from history is that we do not learn anything from history.

66. Some people's darkness is better than other people's light. Job

67. You can no more teach what you have not learned, than you can come back from where you have not been.

68. Old pipes rust out faster than they wear out.

69. Never stir something that stinks!

70. People seldom read the Four Gospels. They read the Fifth Gospel, our lives.

71. We preach better than we live. There is too big a gap between profession and practice.

72. We are writing a Gospel, a chapter a day, by the deeds that we do, by the words that we say. Man reads what we write, whether faithful or true. What is the Gospel, according to you?

73. People don't care how much you know, until they know how much you care.

74. We have not yet learned how we can all live together, but we have learned how to die together.

75. As well as all being *created* equal, it may be that we will all be *cremated* equal.

76. There is more hope today for a self-convicted sinner than a self-conceited saint!

77. Silence is sometimes golden, but other times, it is just plain yellow!

78. Don't do something when you are young that you will be sorry for all of the rest of your life, Ecclesiastes 12: 1.

79. It is better to keep your mouth shut and let people think you are stupid, than to open it and remove all doubt!

80. People seldom, if ever, rise above their leadership. They become like what they see.

81. Jesus came into the world by way of a barn door, and he went out by way of the executioner's chamber.

82. Salvation was lost in the Garden of Eden. It was gained back in the Garden of Gethsemane.

83. There is a lot of *might* in the *mite*!

84. We will answer for three things about our money: how we get it, how we use it, and how we give it, I Corinthians, 4: 2.

85. You are either a missionary or a mission field.

86. Jesus is either Lord of all of your life or none of your life, Colossians 1:18.

87. We are not brothers and sisters because we agree on everything, but we are brothers and sisters because we have the same Father.

88. The problem with being a "living sacrifice," is that we have a tendency to roll off of the alter, Romans 12: 1.

89. It is never out of place for a Christian to pray. It should be like breathing in and breathing out, I Thessalonians 5: 17.

90. Prayer is our high line that leads to our source of power, Almighty God.

91. When is the last time you saw a man die? I Corinthians 11: 23ff.

92. Our task is to convince people that, "God will do what he said he would do," Brother Andrew.

93. It better to give people the benefit of the doubt and be wrong now and then, than to be suspicious of people and be right now and then.

94. Attending church regularly, no more guarantees that you are a Christian, than living in a garage guarantees you are a car.

95. One cannot be considered foolish for being willing to give up that which he cannot keep, in exchange for what he cannot lose.

96. Jesus is far more concerned with comforting the sinner, than condemning the sin, His statement to Peter after His resurrection.

97. Our grand goal in life should be to know God better and love Him more.

98. As mature Christians, we should love God enough to be satisfied with whatever situation we may find ourselves in, I Thessalonians 5: 18.

99. As mature Christians we should love our fellow man enough to not be envious or jealous of their situation, I Corinthians 12: 26.

100. If you run the church like a business it will fail — horizontal, Relying on your own wisdom and strength. If you run the church like a family it will succeed — perpendicular. *"Receiving your wisdom and strength from God,"* Philippians 4: 13.

101. Chicken one day, and feathers the next.

In conclusion, the above Gems are sayings that I have gleaned from many people and sources through the years. They have been helpful in my teaching others. Our prayer is for you to grow to the place in your life, so you can say to those you have discipled in the words of Paul to young Timothy, *"And the things that you have heard from me, among many witnesses, the same commit to faithful men, who will be able to teach others also,"* II Timothy 2: 2.

FROM BOULDER VALLEY CHRISTIAN CHURCH
To
WORLD-WIDE MISSIONS OUTREACH

The time had come when everything was right for us to leave the staff of Boulder Valley Christian Church and give our full attention to fulfilling the mission we had come to Colorado to accomplish. Not only did we have a mission to fulfill, but we knew we would be fulfilled in it.

The elders and minister of the church agreed that it was time for us, like eaglets, to leave the security of the nest provided by the church. The elders agreed to allow us to continue to have an office in the church building and also to continue paying us a salary until we were able to raise the necessary financial support to continue on our own.

We were eager to leave our staff position in a way that would not "burn bridges" so I composed a letter to the Boulder Valley Church Family. It reads as follows:

August 24, 1989

Dear Beloved Boulder Valley Christian Church Family,

"Then Joseph said unto his brothers, 'Please come closer to me,' and they came closer, and he said, 'I am your brother, Joseph, whom you sold into Egypt. For God sent me before you to preserve life.'" Genesis 45: 4-5.

These words describe our coming to Boulder Valley Christian Church, for we believe God's timing was perfect, and that we came at a time when we were able, along with many other faithful Christians and the elders of Boulder Valley Christian Church, to help preserve the life of our wonderful church. Now that mission has been accomplished and we have enjoyed over a year and a half of precious Christian fellowship with Boulder Valley Christian Church.

We have come to a mutual agreement, after many hours of prayerful deliberation, that it is best for all concerned in the long run that we now pursue the original purpose for which we came to Colorado — that is, to establish a dynamic world-wide outreach missions program based here at the University of Colorado, where leadership from every area of life from all over the world will be represented by her graduates for generations to come.

In order to accomplish this goal, it was felt that it is best that we no longer be tied down by a staff position at Boulder Valley Christian Church; therefore, we believe that this letter, to all of you whom we love so dearly, is necessary to clear up any misunderstanding that may arise in regard to our no longer being on your church staff. This will mean we will no longer be able to regularly teach the adult class with Roger Wilson each Lord's Day. But I will be able to come back from time to time as a guest lecturer. I will miss dearly sharing a class with Roger.

There are several areas for which we will covet your prayers that describe what the future will hold for us and our relationship with all the Boulder Valley Christian Church family. First, we will now pursue full time our original purpose for coming to Boulder Valley Christian Church. As suggested earlier, we believe that God sent us here at a very critical time in the life of the church. We are so grateful that we were here when we were needed, but at the same time, we want to point out that we also needed you badly and could not have survived up to now without the support of the church. It should also be remembered that the elders and church in general were under no obligation to us, but graciously opened their arms and hearts to us, and accepted us into the church as a part of the staff.

As I type this letter, we are no longer officially on the staff of Boulder Valley Christian Church. So the second thing I want to mention is the fact that the elders are giving me the necessary time to be away from the church to raise the financial support we will need to continue our ministry with World-Wide Missions Outreach. I have asked for the elder's to continue the church's support through that time, which they have graciously agreed to do. We hope that by January 1, 1990, we can accomplish that goal.

Thirdly, the elders have left the door open for us to receive continued support after January 1, 1990, which we hope will come from the church's newly revived missions program if we are still in need.

Brothers and sisters in Christ, we urge you to get behind the programs presented by our senior minister and elders like you never have before! Even though Normadeene and I will not be officially on the staff of the church, we will still be here during the week as well as whenever we are in town on the Lord's Day. We will remain faithful members of the Boulder Valley Christian Church, striving to be an example to you all. We will have an office in the church building and will be available and eager to serve you in any way possible.

We look forward to having an integral part in the future growth of Boulder Valley Christian Church as we continue to be a Para-ministry of the Christian Churches of Colorado and seek to build God's Kingdom on earth. We love you and appreciate so much all the elders, trustees and people of Boulder Valley Christian Church.

In the words of Habakkuk 1: 5, we believe that God is going to cause such a great thing to happen in the life of our church that we are going to have to see it to believe it.

With much love and affection, part of your family,

Jerry and Normadeene Gibson

Shortly after writing the above letter, we received A CERTIFICATE OF INCORPORATION TO WORLD-WIDE MISSIONS OUTREACH, A NONPROFIT CORPORATION from Natalie Meyer, Colorado's Secretary of State.

* * *

As we contemplate how to recall the events of the past twenty years with World-Wide Missions Outreach, we want to begin by sharing with you the first newsletter we composed after being officially incorporated as a nonprofit religious organization in the State of Colorado. It reads as follows:

WORLD-WIDE MISSIONS OUTREACH
NEWS LETTER

"So shall my word be that goeth forth out of my mouth: it shall not return to me void, but it shall accomplish that which I please, and it shall prosper in the thing whereto I sent it," Isaiah 55: 11.

Dear Christian Friends,

World-Wide Missions Outreach has been actively working on the field for just little over a year. Due to the faithful, prayerful support of Christians like you, we have been able to accomplish far more than we ever dreamed possible to this date.

The purpose of this letter is two-fold. First to give you a financial report, which we deem essential to maintaining our credibility as good stewards of God's money, I Corinthians 4: 2. And secondly to summarize some of the accomplishments of our missionary efforts during our first full year of service, so you can rejoice with us over the many victories that have been won for Jesus Christ due to our combined efforts.

We want to begin by saying that one of the most exciting things that has happened thus far is the addition of Jerry and Lois Clark to our World-Wide Missions staff. Jerry Clark was the head football coach at Cornell College in Mt. Vernon, Iowa for 28 years. He was an elder at the church in Martelle, Iowa. He took an early retirement from his coaching duties and was ordained into the ministry of Jesus Christ this past summer. He has joined us with his wife, Lois, to work specifically as a marriage counselor, and also with Singles, and with the Fellowship of Christian Athletes in our community. He is raising his own financial support through friends and former students who believe in Jerry and Lois and have benefited by their influence through the years while he was coaching and teaching in Iowa.

The most satisfying area of our mission thus-far has been our work with Internationals. As we have told you earlier, many of the nations that cannot be reached by conventional missionary efforts are represented on our campus. Normadeene and I are members of The Board of Directors of Boulder Friends of International Students. As such, we have an open door to establish relationships with every international student that comes to Boulder.

We also serve as host family for both the Economic Institute and the university at large. We work with students from Africa, India, Indonesia, Korea, Taiwan and Mainland China. Mu-Jei-Lin, our first Mainland China student, whom we taught English with the Bible as our text, is now back in China sharing the Gospel he learned from us with his family and country men.

The Internationals we are working with are the "cream of the crop" as far as scholarship goes from these nations, and will be leaders in every area of life when returning as missionaries to their own people.

Normadeene teaches a class every Sunday morning at the Boulder Valley Christian Church, focused on the needs of International students.

Another area that has proven to be very fruitful has been the booth I have established each week in the heart of the UMC, the Student Union for the University of Colorado. Literally hundreds of students, faculty and staff of the university pass by our table. We have a sign, pictured below, that says, "Ask us any questions you have ever had about the Bible." We have touched many lives from every area of campus life through this means.

People constantly attempt to confront us with what they believe to be unanswerable questions, such as, "If your God is such a loving and powerful God, didn't He create a creature that could not sin?" We respond, "He did. We call them animals." The professor who asked the question walked away mumbling to himself, while the students gathered around for a serious discussion about God and His will for their lives.

This past week climaxed our joy in the ministry on the University of Colorado campus. When we arrived a year ago in Colorado, the first person we met outside of Boulder Valley Christian Church was Cliff Mealy, who turned out to be one of the all time great basketball players to come out of the University of Colorado. At this time, he is the only one whose number was retired at the University. He played for the Lakers and Houston Rockets. Through him we also met Viisha Sedlak who is the number one race walker in the world in her class. Our relationship with them developed through the year, and they began attending my Bible class on Sunday morning at Boulder Valley Christian Church as well as the regular worship services conducted by David Roadcup.

We were invited into their homes to present the design and purpose of Christian baptism to them. On Resurrection Sunday morning I had the privilege of baptizing the two of them into Jesus Christ. (Pictures below) They will have an influence on people that most of us could never reach. Oh, the joy from this fruit from our labors! *"God does indeed give the increase."* I Corinthians 3: 7.

MENTORING MENTORS
Matthew 28: l9-20; II Timothy 2: 2

As we contemplated the direction our ministry was taking, we came to realize that everything we had invested our life's energy in up to that time was that of carrying out the Great Commission of Jesus, *"Go therefore and make disciples of all nations, baptizing them in the name of the Father and the Son and the Holy Spirit, teaching them to observe all that I commanded you; and lo, I am with you always, even to the end of the age,"* Matthew 28: 19-20. And also the commission of the Apostle Paul to the young preacher Timothy, *"And the things which you have heard from me in the presence of many witnesses, these entrust to faithful men, who will be able to teach others also,"* II Timothy 2: 2.

There has not been much written about *mentoring* in the past sixty years. The main emphasis has been on *leadership training* in both the secular and religious realms of our society. That is certainly much needed in every area of life. I have often said, Very few people ever rise above their leadership. We become like what we see. We lead by example. The *Achilles heel* of our churches today is an unqualified leadership. Having said all of that, I want to remind you, as I will do often in the remaining chapters of this book, Jesus never called for *leaders* as such. He called for *followers*. His appeal to His disciples was always basically, *"Take up your cross and follow me,"* Matthew 16: 24.

Jesus was the last and the best of a long line of *Peripatetic (walking) teachers,* or *disciple makers*. As they walked they talked, Socrates, Plato and Aristotle were all *walking teachers*. Jesus commanded His followers to become *walking teachers*. He said, *"Make this the habit of your life,"* Like breathing in and breathing out. *"As you go, and wherever you go, make disciples or followers of me."*

It has well been said, "Christ alone can save the world, but Christ cannot save the world alone." That is why His mission was unique to all other *mentors* or *disciple makers.*

It was unique because it was *revealed* in all of its aspects. The word *revelation* is what distinguishes Christianity from all other religions. That is what makes the Holy Bible the only book of its kind. It reveals to man the very mind of God. The English word *religion* comes from the Latin *"religio,"* which means *to bind back.* True religion is that, which *binds men back to God.* All other religions are false!

In many of the early translations of the Bible, Proverbs 29: 18, which is often used to challenge graduating Seniors to look eagerly with a *vision* for the future, is translated, *"Where there is no vision the people perish."* We have no quarrel with that challenge, for to *fail to plan is to plan to fail.* However that is not the true meaning of that word in that passage of Scripture. It would more properly be translated, *"Where there is no revelation from God for His will in our lives, people perish."* It can readily be understood in the words in I Samuel 3: 1, *"Now the boy Samuel was ministering to the LORD before Eli. And word from the LORD was <u>rare</u> in those days, <u>visions</u> were infrequent."*

Jesus' ministry was revealed as to its PURPOSE: *"For the Son of Man has come to seek and to save that which was lost,"* Luke 19:10. It was revealed as to its TASK: *"As the Father has sent me, so send I you,"* John 20:21. And it was revealed as to its message: *"Go into all the world and preach the <u>gospel</u>."* That was His message.

Jesus recognized three things: The lostness of the lost, *"For all have sinned and come short of the glory of God,"* Romans 3: 23; *"The wages of sin is <u>death</u>,"* 6: 23a. The power of the Gospel to save, *"For I am not ashamed of the gospel of Jesus Christ, for it is the power of God unto salvation, to the Jew first and also the Greek,* Romans, 1: 16; *but the gift of God is eternal life through Jesus Christ our Lord,"* Romans 6: 23b; *"And there is salvation in no one else; for there is no other name under heaven that has been given among men, by which we must be saved."* His obligation to save to lost, *"For the Son of man has come to seek and to save that which was lost,"* Luke 1 9: l0.

The Apostle Paul categorically proclaimed the Divine inspiration of the Scriptures. He declared to Timothy, *"<u>All</u> Scripture is inspired by God and profitable for teaching, for reproof, for correction, for training in righteousness; that the man of God may be adequate, equipped for every good work,"* II Timothy 3:16-17.

Radical scholars have often challenged Paul's authority as a genuine apostle of Jesus Christ. That motivated him on several occasions to make it a point to declare to his audience from whom he received his authority. In his letter to the Corinthians he told them where he received the teaching he was about to share with them concerning the proper manner of partaking of the Lord's Supper. He said, *"For I received from the Lord that which I also delivered to you,"* I Corinthians 11: 23. He did the same in his great defense of the resurrection of Jesus Christ from the dead, where he says, *"For I delivered to you as of first importance what I also received,* (from Jesus) *that Christ died for our sins according to the Scriptures, and that He was buried, and that He was raised on the third day according to the Scriptures,"* I Corinthians 15: 3-4.

While I was serving as a campus minister and Emergency dean for the University of Illinois, I reminded a prominent speaker and the audience of campus ministers and professors he was addressing that his claim, that the Apostle Paul did not consider himself to have had any more extra special revelation from God, other than that, which the speaker had, was false. Except for a rabbi in the crowd and me, everyone nodded in agreement. I was compelled to interrupt him and ask him and the nodding in agreement ministers and professors, "Have you heard Paul's words to the Galatians? *"For I would have you know, brethren, that the gospel which was preached by me is not according to man. For I neither received it from man, nor was I taught it, but I received it through a <u>revelation</u> of Jesus Christ,"* Galatians 1: 11-12.

Experiences like that are what motivated me to concentrate most of my time to a ministry of MENTORING MENTORS.

My deepest concern for the men and women I mentor is for them to grow into *mature* "telios" Christians. I want to be sure that after spending four years with me on a weekly basis, they are not same people four years from the time we began to meet together.

My fear of fears is what I have seen in so many churches where I have held special services through the years. The admonition of the Apostle Paul to the Corinthians describes the majority of churches today. This is especially true of "Mega" *Churches,* where it is almost impossible to prepare enough mentors to mentor mentors. He seems to be broken hearted as he admonishes them, *"And I, brethren, could not speak to you as to spiritual (pneumatikos) men, but as to men of flesh, (sarkakos) as to babes in Christ. I gave you milk to drink and not solid food; for you were not yet able to receive it. Indeed, even now you are not yet able, for you are still fleshly. (sarkakos) For since there is jealousy and strife among you, are you not fleshly,* *(sarkakos) and are you not walking like <u>mere</u> <u>men</u>,"* I Corinthians 3: 1-3. *"Mere men,"* what a tragedy? As Christians we are, *"A peculiar people, a chosen generation, a royal priesthood."* II Corinthians 5: 17 - 6: 16. This along with other Scriptures declares that we are the very *"temple of God."* We are the *"Holy of Holies,"* the (*Naos*) the inner sanctuary where the *Shekinah Glory* resides. Unfortunately, there is the "ideal" and the "actual."

I make a concerted effort to begin my mentoring sessions by starting with people where I find them, and not where I want them to be. The following goals, as mentioned before, are kept in mind to help them measure their spiritual growth: *"A desire to know God better and love God more; to love God enough to be satisfied with whatever situation we may find ourselves in; to love my fellow man enough to not be envious or jealous of his or her situation; I must have a desire to be more like Jesus today than yesterday and more like Him tomorrow than today,"* Romans 13: 14; I Corinthians 11: 1; Philippians 1: 21.

Jesus prepared Himself for His mission. He spent thirty years preparing for three years of ministry. When I mentor mentors, my desire is to help prepare them in the same way Jesus prepared Himself for His ministry. I impress upon them that in direct proportion to how we prepare ourselves, God will open avenues of service for us. We must be willing to pay the price of preparation. I have often commented, I would rather see a man or woman die during their first mentoring session than to go out unprepared. It has well been said, "You can no more teach what you have not learned, than you can come back where you have not been!" Please keep these areas of Jesus' preparation in your mind as we examine what the Bible says about measuring one's spiritual growth.

I. JESUS SATURATED HIMSELF WITH THE WORD OF GOD.

    A. Psalm 1: 1-5 describes Jesus' inaugural address. He meditated, *"on God's word both day and night."*

    B. Psalm 119: 11 describes Jesus' defense against Satan when He was tempted. Ephesians 6: 10-18 suggests the same for all of us. The sword of the Spirit is our best defense, Ephesians 6: 17.

    C. Matthew 4: 4-10 Jesus overcame temptation by quoting Scriptures. He never replied, "I think this, or I think that." He always quoted scripture. His reply was *"It is written . . ."* Matthew 4: 4, 7, & 10.

    D. The best answer one can give when someone asks us a question, whenever applicable is, *"Thus saith the Lord . . ."* not, I think this, or I think that.

II. JESUS SPENT MUCH TIME IN FELLOWSHIP AND PRAYER WITH GOD.

    A. Follow one day in the Life of Jesus. He got up early in the morning and found a quiet place to pray, Mark 1: 35. And then after a day that would cause most of us to drop in our tracks, the last thing He did was find a place to pray.

    B. His final words on the cross were a prayer asking His Heavenly Father to forgive those who in ignorance nailed Him to the cruel cross on Golgotha, Luke 23: 34; I Corinthians 2: 8.

    C. It is never out of place for a person to pray. It should be like breathing in and breathing out. Brother Andrews once made a simple, but profound statement when addressing a group of ministers. He said, "Our job is to convince people that God will do what He said He would do." Jesus suggested on one occasion that, *"if we had the faith of a grain of mustard seed, we could move mountain."* Mathew 17: 20 More often than not, we don't have enough faith to move a mustard seed, let alone a mountain.

D. Prayer is our high line that leads to our source of power, Almighty God. We should start out everyday speaking to God first. That sets the tone for the rest of the day. We should pray before we put on our Jesus suits, Romans 13: 14.

III. JESUS TOOK TIME TO LEARN ABOUT PEOPLE AND LOVE THEM.

A. The Samaritan Woman at the well is a classic example of how Jesus crossed all social, racial, economic and religious barriers to learn about people and demonstrate His love for them, John 4: 7-26.

B. The same was true in the case of Zaccheus. He invited Himself to have dinner with Zaccheus. Zaccheus was a despised "Publican" or "tax gatherer" for the Roman occupational government. He was never the same after having Jesus as a guest in his house. How often has Jesus been a guest in your house?

C. The Rich Young Ruler is a classic example of Jesus' unconditional love. Even though Jesus knew the young man had rejected His counsel, the passage in Mark ends with these words, *"And looking at him, Jesus felt a love for him,"* Mark 10: 21.

D. Above all, Jesus was *ENTHUSIASTIC* about His mission. We need to seek out young men and women who emulate the enthusiasm of our Lord Jesus in regard to his purpose, task and message. Enthusiasm comes from the Greek *enthuos,* "God in you." As Christians we are the temple of the Holy Spirit. That implies that God is in us. We should strive to act like that is true.

As we have been suggesting all along, the first thing one must do in order to mentor mentors is to measure our own spiritual growth, and do the same for the young men and women we desire to mentor.

After receiving a commitment from your disciples to strive to meet the goals mentioned earlier and reiterated several times, you must seek out enthusiastic young men and women who will agree to meet with you on a regular basis, ideally for at least four years, men and women who will commit to those grand goals: *love God* enough to be satisfied with whatever situation we might find ourselves in; to *love our fellow man* enough to not be envious of his or her situation; to *know God better* and love Him more; and to *be more like Jesus today* than yesterday, and more like him tomorrow than today.

And then to receive a commitment from them to meet with you on a regular basis for at least four years, after which time they will seek out enthusiastic men and women who desire to become mentors of mentors.

The first thing we do when we meet for the first time is attempt to measure the spiritual growth of our disciples and explain to them that after four years of meeting with them, they will have grown measurably from that time until they are ready to be a mentor of mentors.

Hebrews 5: 11-6: 10 give us a clear picture of what it means to be mature or "perfect" in the Biblical sense of the word *Telios,* which means to be whole, healthy or well in every area of one's life, Matthew 5: 48. Being saved is not just a matter of having our sins forgiven, and when we die, go to heaven. The Greek word *Soterion* implies that we will live a life of service and spiritual growth, reaching many with the message of Christ, and then when we die, we will have laid up much treasure in heaven. Let us consider the "Proofs of Perfection" as found in the Hebrews letter.

The basic signs or marks that distinguish a mature Christian, a (pneumatikos) Christian from a baby, a (sarkakos) Christian, will be found in the next chapter.

PROOF OF PERFECTION

Hebrews 5: 11-6: 10

I recall the words of a professor I had when I attended the University of Minnesota. His name was Bob Ames. We were discussing the problem of good and evil and specifically the inhumanity of man to man. He commented on Pilate's question to Jesus, "What is truth?" He shared with us the story of one of the greatest Greek philosophers during the time of Alexander the Great. His name was Diogenes. The story is told in Geek literature that Diogenes went about in broad daylight and would hold a lighted lantern in the face of a man. People inquired of him, "What are you doing?" He would reply, "I am looking for an honest man!" In response, the townspeople would bring their most respected citizens and parade them in front of Diogenes. On one such occasion, he responded, "I said men, not pigmies!"

Alexander the Great heard of this, now famous, Greek philosopher. It's said that he marched a legion of his soldiers to where Diogenes was living in a barrel. With a loud and authoritative voice Alexander the Great addressed Diogenes in his barrel, "What can I do for you great and renowned philosopher?" To which Diogenes replied, "Step aside you're blocking the light from my barrel!"

We face a similar dilemma today. It is difficult to find an honest man or woman who is mature in his or her walk with Christ, who always speaks the truth, even when it may hurt. Jesus calls for perfection in His inaugural address. He demands, *"Be perfect as your Father in heaven is perfect,"* Matthew 5: 48. Is this possible?

The scripture from the Hebrew letter, featured under the title of this chapter, is a perfect guideline for what it means to be "perfect" in the Biblical sense of the word. As we know, the

Greek word "telios" which is translated "perfect" some times means "to be whole, healthy or well." It can also mean "to be constant," or "to be the same" as opposed to "being hypocritical." We are using it in the context of Paul's admonition to the Corinthian church, referred to earlier, in I Corinthians 3: 1-3. "Telios" means to be a mature Christian, as opposed to being a "babe in Christ."

Jesus calls for "perfection" in His inaugural address in Matthew 5: 48. He says *"Be perfect as your Father in heaven is perfect."* Is this possible? He is not speaking of being free from sin. When one becomes a Christian he "buries" his old sinful nature, Romans 6: 1-6. However, as I John 1: 8-9 says, speaking to Christians, *"If we say we have no sin, we deceive ourselves and the truth is not in us. If we confess our sins, He is faithful and just to forgive our sins, and cleanse us from all unrighteousness."* After we become Christians, we are more apt to commit sins of "omission," rather than sins of "commission." The Book of James speaks of this when it says, *"He that knows what is good and doesn't do it, to him it is sin,"* James 4: 17.

In the Old Testament, the Hebrew word "Ta:mym" is defined as "being whole, complete, blameless, honest, having integrity, and being truthful as demanded by God to be qualified as "a good person" in Micah 6: 8. The question is asked, *"What is good, and what does God require of a man, but <u>to do justice</u>,"* (this requires all of the above attributes mentioned above) *"to love kindness, and walk humbly with God."* It is important to note that one cannot *walk humbly with God,* unless he first *does justice and love kindness.*

The term "Ta:mym" is first found in the Old Testament in Genesis 6: 9. It refers to Noah as "being perfect" in his day. It should be pointed out that in this context it was a comparative word. Compared to others in Noah's day, he was "perfect."

There are three very simple tests to define a "mature" or "perfect" Christian. By following Jesus' example of preparing Himself for His ministry, we, too should be able to reach the goal of being "perfect" in the Biblical sense of the word. Let us briefly examine the words written to us in a letter in Hebrews 5: 11 - 6: 10.

As we read the eleventh verse of the fifth chapter of Hebrews we immediately come face to face with one of the greatest hindrances of Spiritual maturity. The writer says, *"You have become dull of hearing."* In other words, they had stopped listening. His words were going into one ear and out the other. Unfortunately, this is the case with a large percentage of the people we preach to Lord's Day after Lord's Day.

In verse twelve the writer gives the first mark or characteristic of a truly converted Christian, one who has become mature in their walk with Christ.

A mature person must be able to teach others. The Apostle Paul admonishes in II Timothy 2: 2, *"And the things that you have heard from me among many witnesses, the same commit to faithful men, who shall be able to teach others also."* As suggested earlier, this calls for preparation. This first thing we mentioned about Jesus. He prepared Himself for His ministry by "Saturating Himself with a knowledge of God's Word." He could say with the writer in Psalms, *"Thy Word I have hid in my heart so I will not sin against you,"* Psalm 11: 9-11. A mature Christian who is able to teach others recognizes the tremendous truth in the words of Paul to young Timothy, *"All scripture is inspired of God, and is profitable for teaching, for reproof, for correction, for training in righteousness; that the man of God may be adequate, equipped for every good work,"* II Timothy 3: 16-17. Therefore, he is willing to further heed Paul's admonition to: *"Study to show yourself approved unto God as a workman that does not need to be ashamed, handling accurately the word of truth,"* II Timothy 2: 15.

The second mark of a mature Christian is the result of his knowledge of good and evil, Psalm 119: 11. He is immediately able discern between the two, due to his keen knowledge of the Bible. A mature Christian doesn't even have to think about it. He immediately recognizes right from wrong, and acts accordingly. Paul admonishes, *"Flee from fornication,"* I Corinthians 6: 18. Run from it! Make this the habit of your life. Just as Joseph ran from Potiphar's wife, we must run from a compromise situation. As one man suggested, "Joseph took care of his character, and left his reputation up to God." We must do the same, Hebrews 5: 14.

The third mark of a mature Christian is found in Hebrews 6: 10. A mature Christian is an example of love and service. *"For God is not unjust so as to forget your work, and the love, which you have shown toward His name, in having ministered and in still ministering to the saints."* Once again, this is the "Fifth Gospel," which we speak of so often. The greatest sermon is still, the life we live, I Corinthians 11: 1.

There isn't any Christianity outside of service. Jesus set the example of being a servant when He said, *"I came not to be served, but to serve,"* He really is the, "Suffering Servant" described in chapter 53 of Isaiah.

\

MENTORING FOR MARRIAGE

If we start out right, we are more apt to end up right. Perhaps as much as three-quarters of the time we spend mentoring young men and women is spent with a desire to help them achieve the maximum amount of happiness in their lives. The *Religious* aspect of our relationship is of first importance. It has to do with having the same sense of values as to what is right and wrong. The basic religious principles found in the Bible must be our measuring stick in this area of our relationship. The principles of honesty and integrity are essential here.

Outside of the religious aspect of our lives, the next most important area for true fulfillment and happiness is the *Romantic* aspect of our relationship. That is why the Apostle Paul gives so much attention to this subject in the Seventh Chapter of First Corinthians. The religious area of marriage demands "Agape" type love. That is, "commanded" love. However, the "romantic" aspect of marriage demands "Phileo" type love. This cannot be commanded, as it is subjective, and has to do with chemistry. In our ministry we have found that some young people, especially young women, are willing to sacrifice this aspect of marriage in order to find a man who satisfies the *Religious* aspect of marriage for them. It is very difficult for one to find a truly dedicated Christian in this day and age. That is a mistake that must be avoided, as it may cause some serious problems in the future. People often ask me to define the *Religious* aspect of marriage. The best I can do is as follows:

> Love is a funny thing shaped like a lizard,
> It climbs down your throat and grabs at your gizzard.

Many people have the *Religious* aspect in their relationship, and they have the *Romantic* aspect in their relationship, but their marriages are still not "heaven on earth." Perhaps the most important aspect of marriage is the *friendship* aspect of marriage. Your husband or wife must be your friend before they are your lover. Normadeene is my best friend. I am her best friend. That is the main reason for our sixty years of marriage has been a "heaven on earth" experience. The honeymoon need never be over.

Because of the need to have these three aspects friendship, romance and religion, in the marriage relationship, we go to great lengths to prepare people to cope with the many problems that may confront them after they are married. It has well been said to be forewarned is to be forearmed. These are the three basic aspects in the marriage relationship that will determine whether a person experiences "heaven on earth" or seemingly "hell on earth," in his or her marriage.

We give the following "Marriage Compatibility Questionnaire" as a part of our counseling program for those who desire to have us officiate at their wedding ceremony. It was designed to help avoid many unseen dangers and pitfalls that may confront married couples in their future.

MARRIAGE COMPATIBILITY QUESTIONAIRE

Please indicate your choice with a check mark for the best answer for each question:

1. A marriage should be performed in a respectful setting for which of the following reasons:

    ( ) a. Because people expect it.
    ( ) b. The ceremony is more impressive in a respectful setting.
    ( ) c. Marriage is a sacred matter.
    ( ) d. It makes for more lasting marriages.

2. What is the best evidence that a man and woman are genuinely in love?

    ( ) a. They feel a strong physical attraction to each other.
    ( ) b. They want to be with one another all of the time.
    ( ) c. They like to do the same things together.
    ( ) d. They have strong feelings of affection along with common interests and ideals.

3. What keeps marriage love growing?

    ( ) a. A romantic spirit.
    ( ) b. Financial success.
    ( ) c. Spending most of your time together.
    ( ) d. A desire to make your marriage partner happy.

4. What is the most frequent cause of divorce?

    ( ) a. Sexual incompatibility.
    ( ) b. Money troubles.
    ( ) c. Inability to communicate with each other.
    ( ) d. Immaturity and emotional instability.

5. How important is the sex relationship in marriage?

    ( ) a. It is not too important if other aspects of the marriage are satisfactory.
    ( ) b. It is the most important aspect of marriage.
    ( ) c. It can contribute a great deal of happiness or unhappiness.
    ( ) d. Its importance is often exaggerated.

6. How important is complete faithfulness to each other?

    ( ) a. Most persons are unfaithful at some time during their marriage.
    ( ) b. The success of marriage depends upon complete faithfulness.

( ) c. An occasional lapse need not be too serious.
( ) d. It is unreasonable to expect complete faithfulness.

7. What is your attitude toward divorce?

   ( ) a. Divorce is a convenient way out of an unhappy marriage
   ( ) b. In some cases, divorce is the only solution to an unhappy marriage.
   ( ) c. Divorce is a sin and must always be avoided.
   ( ) d. Many divorces could be avoided if problems are faced realistically and in time.

8. How serious are disagreements in marriage?

   ( ) a. Most couples have them.
   ( ) b. Well-adjusted couples never disagree.
   ( ) c. Disagreements handled in the right way can lead to greater understanding and love.
   ( ) d. Constant disagreements means the marriage has failed.

9. When a husband and wife have a serious disagreement they cannot work out by themselves, what should they do?

   ( ) a. Try separation for a while.
   ( ) b. Talk it over with a professional person (doctor, minister, or counselor).
   ( ) c. Talk it over with friends or relatives.
   ( ) d. Keep arguing until one gives in.

10. What is the best way to develop understanding when there are disagreements?

    ( ) a. Consult a book on marriage problems.
    ( ) b. Try to talk the matter over calmly and objectively.
    ( ) c. Just keep quiet and refuse to discuss the matter.
    ( ) d. Stand firmly for your opinions ands convictions.
    ( ) e. Try to hear what the other person is really saying.

11. What attitude should one take toward his or her in-laws?

    ( ) a. Try to accept and appreciate them.
    ( ) b. Avoid having too much to do with them.
    ( ) c. Insist they keep out of the affairs between husband and wife.
    ( ) d. Draw up some rules regarding the relationship.

12. What is the best living arrangement for a newly-married couple?

    ( ) a. Live with the parents of one or the other until they can afford a place of their own.

( ) b. Live by themselves, even if it must be a rented room.
( ) c. Make their permanent home near the parents of one or the other.
( ) d. Start buying a house, regardless of the cost.

13. What financial agreements should a husband and wife have?

    ( ) a. Let the wife take care of all money matters.
    ( ) b. Let the husband take care of all money matters.
    ( ) c. Let the husband and wife pool their resources, draw up their own budget, and decide on expenditures together.
    ( ) d. Decide these matters as problems arise.
    ( ) e. Have a lawyer draw a mutually agreed upon pre-nuptial agreement.

14. When should both husband and wife work?

    ( ) a. When it is agreeable to both.
    ( ) b. Only when it is a financial necessity.
    ( ) c. Until they have established themselves financially.
    ( ) d. Never.

15. How important are children in marriage?

    ( ) a. They bring the major satisfying fulfillment to marriage.
    ( ) b. They are not too important to happiness in marriage.
    ( ) c. One should not have children unless one can afford them.
    ( ) d. The more children, the more satisfying the marriage becomes.

16. What is your attitude toward birth control?

    ( ) a. It interferes with God's plan.
    ( ) b. It is a proper means of avoiding the conception of children.
    ( ) c. It is an acceptable means of planing one's family.
    ( ) d. It is proper only if non-artificial methods are used.

17. How important is religion in marriage?

    ( ) a. It is important only if one or both members are members of a church.
    ( ) b. It gives the marriage a better chance of lasting
    ( ) c. We can only attain the highest goals in life and in marriage with the help of God and the practice of Biblical moral and ethical principles.
    ( ) d. It is important only after children arrive in the home.

18. What kind of security should a couple have in establishing their home and life together? (Number in order of importance.)

( ) a. Money in the bank or Invested stocks.
( ) b. Steady income.
( ) c. Life Insurance.
( ) d. Complete health examination.
( ) e. Ownership of property.
( ) f. Be reasonably free of debt. (Home furnishing, car, doctors bills, etc.)
( ) g. Health and hospital insurance.

Through the years, I have made several additions and modifications of the questions asked on this exam. Unfortunately, this has been necessary due to the drastic change in the mindset of our world in regard to moral and ethical values.

Marriage is no longer a covenant between two people and God. In the minds of many it is just a "legal contract" that can be terminated by the slightest whim of either partner involved. God is completely left out. "For richer or poorer, for better or worse" have become platitudes not to be taken too seriously. I personally make it a point to impress upon those I counsel and often times officiate at their weddings that vows are not to be taken lightly. I take great pains to point out the example of Jephthah in ninth chapter of the Book of Judges, who went to great extremes to fulfill the vow he made to God, even though it may have cost him the life of his only daughter. That may be an extreme example, but it is important that we start somewhere to impress upon those desiring to be married the fact that marriage in God's eyes is a life time commitment.

The fact that if we start out right, we are much more apt to end up right is the main reason for giving candidates for marriage my "Marriage Compatibility Exam." Our prayer is that as you read this book you will use this chapter as an opportunity to re-evaluate your marriage relationship as well as help you counsel your loved ones who may be about to enter into this second most important decision in life. One's decision to accept Jesus Christ as their Lord and Savior is of course, number one and it is: ***the key that unlocks the door to "heaven on earth marriage."***

OUR LEGACY

Thinking back over the years, there have been several outstanding individuals we have had the privilege of mentoring. They take us back as far as the middle nineteen fifties. Some of them were students of mine when I was a professor at Minnesota Bible College. Some were my students in Ghana Christian College. Others were a part of our campus ministry at the University of Illinois. Others attended Mid-South Christian College when I was the President there. And still others are a result of our ministry at the University of Colorado, which is an ongoing mentoring ministry. Most of them have remained faithful to their calling, the effective call, being the answered call. However, as is always the case there are a few who were unable to continue their work for the Lord. The Apostle Paul experienced this same disappointment during his mentoring ministry, *"For Demas has forsaken me, having loved this present world,"* II Timothy 4: 10.

I want to begin by apologizing to the many that I will not be able to recall at this time. I will attempt to present classic examples of those who Normadeene and I have mentored through the years. Many of them have been very successful in their vocations and avocations, and are now building their own legacy of those they have mentored.

Before coming to Colorado, our mentoring was most often not done on a regularly scheduled weekly basis. Our mentoring was mostly to large groups, such as The Fellowship of Christian Athletes, various university athletic teams and religious studies classes at the university or Bible Colleges where I taught.

At the risk of repeating myself, I want to point out two very important principles that we kept in mind long before we moved to Colorado. These principles paid great dividends in the lives of many of my students in Minnesota, as well as the young men and women we worked with at Illinois University, and at Mid-South Christian College.

The first principle is to start with people where you find them, not where you want them to be. As we looked at young people through Jesus' eyes and not our own, we could see great potential for their future if they received the right guidance and motivation to accomplish the full potential in their lives. Also, it is important to emphasize that it is the "long haul" and not "the short haul" that counts. We repeated over and over that there are three words necessary for success, "Work, work, work!" We pointed out that "the satisfaction will be worth the sacrifice." And "If it doesn't cost anything — it is not worth anything." We appreciate what we pay for — the higher the price, the greater the value."

Jeff and Mark Hollenbach are cases in point. Both of them came to the University of Illinois with great athletic potential. Due to an early injury on the football practice field, Mark was never able to realize his dreams or reach his full potential as a football player. However, Mark picked himself up off of the hospital bed and determined to accomplish something great in his life. It wasn't easy. He was an All-American Athlete in every sense of the word out of high school. He had great expectations for himself and so did his family and many others. When those dreams were dashed, he did not sit around and feel sorry for himself. He enrolled in every one of the Bible credit courses I taught at the university and kept up his grades for his secular degree from the university. By the time he graduated, he was grounded well enough in the Bible to be hired as my Youth Minister at the Webber Street Church in Urbana. From there he attended Lincoln Christian Seminary where he received his Masters Degree and became an excellent teacher and preacher of God's Word. He accepted a position in Mesa Arizona with

Central Christian Church where Le Roy Lawson was the senior minister at the time. He served in various areas of ministry at Central Church for more than twenty years. While ministering there, he met his wife Debbie, who holds a Doctorate degree in music. They are a powerful team in the ministry of our Lord.

After some time, Mark decided he would like to take a "shot" so to speak, in the preaching ministry. He was hired by a church close to his home town in Pennsylvania. After a period of time, Central Christian in Mesa found it was impossible to replace him, as he had skills and a personality that were vital to the spiritual health of the church.

After consulting with Debbie, they agreed they had accomplished most of what they desired to accomplish in Pennsylvania. So they returned to Central Christian Church in Mesa, Arizona where they are enjoying a second tour of duty in the ministry there.

Mark Hollenbach one of our legacies from our ministry at Illinois University.

Jeff Hollenbach (Mark's brother) and Jeff's wife, Libbi, are also a part of our legacy for the University of Illinois. Jeff was the President of our Fellowship of Christian Athletes chapter there. He was voted as "Most Valuable Player" by his coaches and teammates after his senior year of playing "Quarterback" for Illinois' football team. He was also honored by the Fellowship of Athletes as Co-recipient of "The College Christian Athlete of the Year Award" along with Neal Jeffrey. The football coach from Baylor University was there and I believe that his name was Grant Teaff. Roger Staubach of Navy and later on, Dallas Cowboy fame, received the award for the Professional athletes that year. I recall how honored I felt sitting with Jeff, Roger, Coach Tom Landry, and Allen "the horse" Ameche that night in the banquet hall of the Traders Nationals Life Building in Kansas City, Missouri, where FCA was headquartered at the time. Now it's located across from Royal's Stadium in a very beautiful campus complex. As I recall, Jeff's father was there that night along with many other dignitaries.

While at the University of Illinois, Jeff's girl friend from his high school days, back in Pennsylvania, graduated from Goshen College in Indiana and moved to Illinois where she became a school teacher. Jeff and Libby became engaged, and later on I had the privilege of officiating at their wedding ceremony in Bloomburg, Pennsylvania.

Not long after they were married they moved to Northern New Mexico and worked with a Native American High school near Farmington. Jeff served as basketball coach for the women's basketball team. However, the most important thing they accomplished was to preach "the fifth gospel" with their lives. As suggested earlier, very few people read the "Four Gospels." Our lives are the greatest sermon we can preach. For a short time Jeff ministered in a church near his home town of Perkasi, Pennsylvania, and was honored by becoming the head football coach at the high school where he played when his father was a teacher and coach and also Athletic Director for a time.

You can see that the Hollenbach brothers are two of the finest legacies from our campus ministry in Illinois.

We might add that Libby and Jeff's family has followed in the steps of their parents. Mark and Debbi have two daughters who are also fine Christian young women.

For the past few years Jeff and Libby' son, Sam followed in Jeff's footsteps as a quarterback. He played for the University of Maryland, and was their starting quarterback in his last year there. He led them to a post season bowl game. He is an on fire Christian who gives God all of the glory for every success he had as a football player. As I write this story, he is in line to possibly play professional football for the Pittsburgh Steelers. He was fortunate to have met an excellent young man, Matt Nichols from Navigators. He was a spiritual rock for Sam through his years at the University of Maryland.

Danny and Torri Beaver are another glowing example of the influence Jeff and Mark Hollenbach had one their fellow athletes. Danny was a "walk on" field goal kicker for the "Fighting Illini" football team. I should mention, that due to an unfortunate controversy over the University of Illinois' name, "Fighting Illini" and mascot, "Chief Illiniwick," which some claimed to be an insult and racist reflection on the Native American Indians, the university was forced, by legal action, to discontinue the use of that long time beloved traditional name. We wonder what affect that may have on the Athletic teams the university puts on the field. Danny was a part of a missionary family in Central Africa. He was honored upon graduation as an All-American field goal kicker. He and his family have spent the past twenty five or so years of their lives as missionaries in the Philippine Islands where they have made a tremendous impact for Christ all over that area of the world. He has been active in taking athletic teams to various countries where he and his athletes give powerful testimonies to the teams they play, not only by demonstrating Christian principles of sportsmanship, but also by enthusiastic verbal confessions as to what Jesus Christ means to them. There is much more I could say on their behalf, but I am confident you can understand why we are proud of having the Beaver family as a part of our "Living legacy."

It is important that we mention that one of Danny Beaver's legacies is Danny Brown from Gibson City, Illinois. God has seen fit to bring Danny's family back into Normadeene's and my life in the past few years. Danny Beaver led Danny Brown away from the "party like atmosphere" at the University of Illinois to our Fellowship of Christian Athletes meetings where I first met him. He became an active, devout Christian young man who was honored by being elected the President of The Fellowship of Christian Athletes. He transferred from Illinois to Mississippi State University where he carried his love for Jesus with him. Since we were reunited, Danny and his Christian family have devoted their time, money and effort to various mission fields. Like the Apostle Paul, Danny "makes tents" so to speak by selling real estate. The money he gains from this "avocation," his vocation is being a Christian, is used to finance the missionary journeys he his wife Cheryl and their family make each year. Danny's son Danny Jr. and his lovely Christian wife Elizabeth are very special. Danny has attended Bible College, and is an excellent preacher. He and Elizabeth are also talented musicians who have an impact for Christ through their music ministry also. The entire Brown family is one to be admired. During a recent program the Brown family conducted at the Harvest Church in Boulder, Colorado, each member of the Brown family gave a personal testimony. Their youngest daughter, Ann Taylor, "stole the show" with the most powerful testimony.

I recently had the privilege of traveling to Orlando, Florida, where the Brown's now live to speak to the church where the Browns attend. It was a rewarding experience, and a tremendous honor to hear the Browns refer to themselves as being a part of my legacy through Danny Beaver.

Doug and Sue Kleber are also precious legacies from our ministry at the University of Illinois. I would like to have Doug and Sue write their own story, as their journey with the Lord is one of the most remarkable we have known. They know what it means to appreciate good news after experiencing some very bad news. Just as Joseph was not put into the pit and later in prison in Egypt, but God put him there, Doug Kleber found himself in prison where he learned some valuable lessons on the importance of making the right decisions in life.

Doug was an outstanding athlete. He could have played both professional baseball and also football had he not suffered a career ending injury while playing for, I believe, the Cleveland Browns football team. He and Sue are spending most of their time mentoring young men and women, helping them to never make any important decisions in life without first seeking God's will in the matter. He and Sue can reach both men and women who most of us could not reach because he can relate to them, having had first hand experiences in the results of making wrong choices, whether a matter or an error in judgment or an error in heart. They have wonderful Christian children who are an excellent example of what it is to be like Jesus.

We want to mention Rick "Scuz" Schweig, because our relationship has been revived after more than a quarter of a century. Rick came to the University and soon became involved in The Fellowship of Christian Athletes. He found a personal relationship with Christ through the preaching and teaching he received from me as well as the testimonies of others. He established close ties with many of the athletes who attended the FCA meetings. Doug Kleber, Jeff and Mark Hollenbach, Jeff Goldberg and Steve Schneider were some of the young men Rick connected with.

Unfortunately, while Rick was still very young he became involved in a group that set itself apart from the rest of us. Someone in the group received what they called a "prophetic" message instructing Rick to marry a young lady in their group. I advised him to go very slow and not rush into something he may be sorry for the rest of his life. However, due to the insistence of the group's leaders, he married the young woman. The marriage only lasted a short time. He left the group under very unpleasant circumstances and has been single ever since.

Rick became a very successful businessman in the Chicago area. He started a mentoring ministry for many young men he knew through his business connections. He insisted they "keep the main thing, the main thing" as he grilled the fundamental principles of the Bible into their minds. He has a personal legacy of which he may rightly be proud.

We received a phone call from him about two years ago. He was able to get our telephone number from the Hollenbachs, I believe. He informed us that he had clients in the Denver area, and would like to meet with us some time when he was in Denver. Not long after, we had the privilege of hosting Rick in our home in Lafayette. It proved to be a delightful experience. He expressed his desire to assist us in the ministry of World-Wide Missions Outreach in any way possible. Since that time he has joined me in my mentoring sessions at the university as well as at Denny's restaurant in Boulder on a Saturday morning. He is very interested in providing some kind of assistance to Albus Brooks, the director of Young Life in Central Denver. Rick has a passion for lost souls and takes advantage of every opportunity afforded him to tell others about the saving power of Jesus Christ.

Since moving to Colorado, and working with students at the University of Colorado, we find the circumstances here are ideal for a mentoring ministry. It is in a place where a great number of students attend meetings and come to hear special speakers throughout the week. We have established ourselves, with the blessings of the University Memorial Center work staff. We have influenced many of them for Christ during the twenty years we have been on campus. We have baptized some of them into Christ. We have a special corner adjacent to the

Glen Miller Ballroom where our presence is easily noticed by anyone who comes to that part of the building. On several occasions we have been displaced from our regular corner of meeting. In the past semester, during "Career Day" events, being displaced led to one of the most challenging opportunities we have faced in Colorado. It was during these times we regularly went to local restaurants. I will share that very remarkable experience in this book. I may well have called it a "Providential" experience, as I am sure you will agree with that assessment after you hear about it.

We met regularly in several restaurants in the Boulder area. God has opened some very interesting opportunities to bring comfort and hope to people from all walks of life, from all over the world. As Donasian Okoula, Tony Rettig, Jay Keeney, Paul Wise and I discussed how to settle disputes in the church family, we were interrupted by a man named James who said he was facing a very difficult time in his life. His son Xavier, was attending the University of Colorado and was in need of his father's guidance. James told us Xavier and he were from San Antonio, Texas. He was praying for a solution to his son's problem and had overheard our conversation. He said that what I had been teaching the men I was mentoring was an immediate answer to his prayers. We prayed for him and his son's situation right there on the spot. We have established a warm relationship. This is one of many such providential meetings I have experienced at restaurants.

ANGELS IN ENGLAND

I want to share with you some experiences we have had in the Twenty-first Century that demonstrate the fact that God still surrounds us with His Guardian Angels. He uses them to see to it that we, *"are not tested beyond what we are able to bear . . ."* I Corinthians 10: 13.

As I turned eighty in May of 2006, our children thought that was a milestone in my life that was worthy of a special celebration. They asked me if there was any place I would like to travel to. I told them I had always desired to visit Scotland, as my ancestors on my father's side were from Scotland. They took care of all of the arrangements. Normadeene and I took care of all of the necessary business at home, including being sure to take along the prescription drugs and other medications to last us until we got back home in Colorado. We did not even think of double checking the dosages, trusting our doctor and pharmacist to do so. We drove to Phoenix, and a day later, we were on a plane headed for Scotland. Little did we know what was in store for us.

Soon after arriving in England I noticed that I was more tired than usual. It was not "jet lag" kind of tired. We took a train from London to Scotland. It was a beautiful trip that allowed us to see the country-side. We marveled at the well-kept farms with cattle and sheep grazing in the lush fields of hay. As we got closer to Scotland, much of the railway was along the ocean coast.

Soon after we checked into our hotel, I noticed that the skin on my legs was beginning to turn black and blue. I thought I may have bruised my legs somehow without knowing it. One particular spot on my knee was very painful. I should have immediately checked into the emergency room of a hospital. However, I did not want to spoil it for everyone else, so I decided to wait until we got back to Phoenix. I found out later that that decision almost cost me my life.

After an enjoyable time in Edenborough, we took the train back to London. At the time I became black and blue all over my body. I still had not gained back my strength.

A visit to the British Museum was a must before we went back home. We spent time there on our way to Africa in 1966, so the museum held many fond memories for us. Normadeene's knee began to bother her to the point that she could not walk without much pain, and I pushed her through the halls of the British Museum in a wheelchair.

Normadeene needed to go to the restroom. They told us there was a restroom especially for people who were handicapped. I pushed her to the restroom and waited for her to come out. When she came out I decided I should take advantage of the restroom, even though it was a women's restroom. I asked Normadeene to stand guard outside the door. The first thing I did upon entering the rest room was to take off the money-belt I had strapped around my waste. As I got ready to leave, I mistakenly pulled a cord that set off an alarm. I did not want to be caught in a women's restroom, so I hurried out. We continued on our way being careful not to miss anything in the museum.

Noremadeene told me that she was hungry so I pushed her to the Food Court. She sat down at a table and started a conversation with a couple of ladies who worked at the museum. I asked her what she wanted to eat. I then reached for my money belt. It was gone! In my hurry to get out of the women's restroom, I had left it there. I was seized with a sudden rush of panic. Everything we needed to continue our journey back home to America was in that little, green money belt! I am talking about our passports, plane tickets, and all of our money! I left

Normadeene and ran back the rest room hoping the little green money belt would still be there. That was wishful thinking. It was not there. I told a security guard about my dilemma. He said that he doubted I would ever find it, but told me where the Lost and Found department was located.

I ran to the Lost and Found and frantically asked them if anyone had turned it in. They said, "No, not yet." They told me that they would make some phone calls to see if it had been found but had not yet arrived at the Lost and Found. Jesus said, "Watch and pray." I waited and prayed. I have often said, "We don't learn patience. We must practice patience." At that time, I was doing both.

Once again, my angel was watching over me. A lady came out of a room and said, "I found this on a table. Is it yours?" There before my anxious eyes was my little green money belt. They told me that I had no idea how rare it was to get something back like that. Everything was still intact. They went on to tell me that one of the major problems at the museum was to protect people from pick pockets and other savory characters.

I Corinthians 10: 13 comes to my mind. Once again, God realized that along with my physical condition, it would have been too much for me to bear if I had to face the difficulties that would come from losing our passports, plane tickets and money.

We waited a long time at the airport. It was a long flight home. We were in cramped conditions. My legs and the rest of my body had also become black and blue. I did not realize how important it was not to fall or bump into anything on the airplane.

When we arrived at the airport in Phoenix we immediately went to baggage claim, as I knew I had to do something about my physical condition. Unfortunately, somebody had mistaken a piece of Becky's luggage for theirs, and she had to spend time trying to track the woman down. When we finally got outside, I decided to call my doctor. When I told him of my condition he said that I was in serious trouble and should go immediately to a hospital emergency room. Somehow, we did not realize the seriousness of my situation. We leisurely drove to Becky and Mark's house and unloaded our luggage, left Laura and Carly, and drove to the nearest hospital which happened to be, not too far away, in Mesa. I might mention that it was hot! The temperature was still well above 100 degrees well into the night.

We arrived at the hospital around 8:30 p.m. I checked into the emergency room where I filled out a number of questionnaires. We found a place to sit in the waiting room. It proved to be, perhaps, the longest wait in my life. We waited there until about 3 a.m. in the morning before a doctor would see me. While we were waiting, Becky lost her patience. She yelled, "My father is very sick. He is an old man. He has been waiting far too long to be acceptable." She was told that sometimes people have had to wait a whole day before they were seen.

When a doctor finally showed up, he ordered a blood test. They were unable to draw any blood. He exclaimed, "It is a miracle! We cannot measure his blood. He has no blood!" The nurses came running and said, "This old man walked in here dressed in a suit and tie when he should be dead."

They immediately put me on transfusions that lasted all day long. They told Normadeene to go home and bring back things that I would need, as they needed too monitor my blood very carefully. They expected me to be there for several days.

The next morning the doctor said there was another miracle. He told me my blood was back to normal and I could go home.

While this was happening, Normadeene was praying that I would not have to stay in the hospital very long. While she was praying I called Mark and told him the good news. In less than an hour later I was checked out of the hospital and both of us were starving for some good food. We drove directly to Denny's restaurant where Normadeene devoured biscuits and gravy, which she hardly ever ate. She said it was the best thing she had eaten for a long time.

Two days later we drove north for Colorado. We had been away for about two weeks and knew we had a lot of catching up to do when we got back home. Soon, after we arrived back home, I started to have the same problem again. My doctor checked my blood and found that it was too thin. I usually took two milligrams of the blood thinner, Cumadin on Sunday, Monday, Wednesday and Friday. On Tuesday and Thursday I took two and a half milligrams and did not take any on Saturday. My doctor's nurse called and said I should not take any Cumadin on Monday and Wednesday and then continue my regular two milligrams on Friday. I happened to have my bottle of Cumadin in front of me. I looked at it and could not believe what I saw. It said it contained thirty *FIVE MILLIGRAM* tablets of Cumadin! Without realizing it, I had been taking more than double the amount of Cumadin I was supposed to be taking. There had been a mistake in the dosage prescribed. That mistake almost cost my life. I asked the doctor how I managed to survive without blood. He said that somehow my heart was able to produce enough fluid to keep pumping. I am convinced my angel kept my heart beating.

People have asked me, "Did your doctor write out the wrong prescription? Or was it the pharmacist's fault?" I tell them, "I am not interested in *who* split the log. I am only concerned with *putting it back together."*

THOSE AMAZING TWENTY-THREE YEARS

On November 1, 2010 we completed twenty-three amazing years of ministry. As I begin this chapter, we recall many significant milestones in our lives. We celebrated my eighty-fourth birthday on May 4th, and Normadeene's eighty-second birthday on May 26th. Before that we experienced some very serious health issues. Normadeene was diagnosed with breast cancer. Following surgery, which revealed the cancer had not spread, she underwent a series of twenty-eight radiation treatments. During this same period of time I suffered a badly infected left thumb. It is believe that I was bitten by a Brown Recluse spider. Now all of that is behind us. We thank God for the many prayers that were offered up in our behalf. But most of all, we thank God for His healing hand, as we believe that all healing is "Divine" healing.

As amazing as our twenty plus years of ministry in Colorado may be, our children believe that being married for sixty-one years is even more amazing! June l3, 2010 marked that milestone in our lives. Our children planned a gala celebration on the third of July at the Boulderado Hotel in Boulder. They mailed out special invitations to many special friends to join us for our Sixtieth-first Anniversary celebration. They limited the invitations to people whom they thought would be able to attend.

I put together a brief summery of what happened that day, and the names of those who participated in a special way, along with a list of many who honored us by their presence. Normadeene and I both agree that the highlight of the celebration was our two granddaughters, Laura and Charlotte Henriksen dedicating a special song, accompanied by Laura's guitar expressing their love for us.

THE LAST HURRAH

At the beginning of 2010 Normadeene and I were informed that we should seriously consider closing our ministry in Colorado, and move closer to a family member. It was suggested that we needed some immediate family closer to us in case of an emergency situation. At first we were very much opposed to the suggestion. But after further contemplation on the subject, we decided to think about such a move more seriously. This would soon mark the beginning of what we consider to be our "Last Hurrah." As difficult as it was we found ourselves packing to move to Mesa, Arizona, where our son-in-law and daughter, Mark and Becky Henriksen built a brand new house for us, swimming pool and all to move into as our new home.

Our long time friend and Treasurer for our mission organized a special Sunday afternoon farewell for us at Second Baptist Church in Boulder. It was a "gala" event. It was attended by well over a hundred people whose lives we had touched in our twenty-three years of ministry in Colorado. The Christian Church of Broomfield, our home church honored us in the same way. It isn't easy to say goodbye to people who love you and you love them.

The problem we faced was getting packed and making arrangements to move. We found that the biggest problem we would face is the fact that even though we considered ourselves to be "collectors" during the years we lived in the house owned by our dear friends, Steve and Barb Taniguchi, We found ourselves to be "hoarders" and not "collectors." That was not easy for us to own up to.

THE FRUIT OF OUR LABOR

As we look back at the joy of ministering to hundreds of college students during the past sixty plus years, the greatest joy we had was that of helping men and women to "put on their Jesus suits." Galatians 3: 27 teaches us "As many of you who have been baptized into Christ have clothed yourself with Christ."

I have decided to include some beautiful pictures of some of those with whom we shared this joy. I have decided not to try and identify all of them by name, as there were so many. The following is a partial list of those I had the privilege of baptizing during our first few years in Colorado:

Cliff Mealy	James Avril
Viisha Sedlack.	Kyle Smith
Rochellel Quackenbush	Jerry Smith.
Jim Quackenbush	Russell Trice
Sharon Trice	James Avril
Bill Everett	Kirston Everett.
Reza Mahlouji.	Lisa Graff.
Carol Jahnlouji.	Leslie Douglas
Qi Chang.	Mike McFadden.
Doris Pletcher.	Hanna Hopper.
Bryan Staltenberg.	Scott Carson.
Darcy Ballentine.	Tennyson McCarty.

Matt Hall.

Gwen Smith (Pine River)

Jamie Engelking

Margarette Fuhr.

James Messmer.

Kristi Rexford.

Nathan Wright.

Jeff Grigsby.

Judy Patasky.

Jeff Green.

Sam Baker.

Jake Baker.

Jenny Roulier.

Craig Ochs.

Jessi Ochs.

Tony Rettig.

Zack Crandall.

Klylie McCarille.

Joey Bocci.

Josh Plumley.

Cameron Harrison.

Sara Ordway Klatt.

Kelly Campbell.

Craig Melville.

Kristin Dorsch.

Julie Connely.

Clare Loveman.

Thomas Louden.

Lindsey Reynolds.

Di Spencer

Phil Dittberner

Marian Ditberner

Kate Fagen

Whitney Law

Tera Bjorklund

Donasian Okoula

Erin Lockhart

Mariko Bliss.

Anadee Johnson

Sarah Leni.

Andrea Garcia

Joseph Garcia

Ben Sprague

Tyler McNamera

Jerry Knutson	Mark Rockefeller
Jay Keeney	Shawna Keeney
Kelly Kenney	Eric Strand
Laura Strand	John Arvidson
Virginia Arvidson	Brad Gomer
Britt Gomer	Mark Smith
Shana Jarvis.	Clare Rockefeller
Steve Mertz.	Gary Howe

There are eighty-four new born babes in Christ who have put on their Jesus suits in the above list. I realize there are many who I baptized that are not included in the above list. If you are one of them, please forgive me.

When possible, I would like you to notice the facial expressions of some before and some after their baptism. Jesus declared in John 3: 5 "You must be born again." How is that possible? Are we expected to crawl back into our mother's womb? No, that would be impossible. Romans 6: 3-5 describes this well. "Or do you not know (This is a "litotes" in the Greek language. It means, "This is something you are supposed to know!" He goes on to say, *"that all of you who have been baptized into Christ Jesus have been baptized into His death? Therefore we have been buried with him through baptism into death, in order that as Christ was raised from the dead through the glory of the Father, we too might walk in newness of life. For if we have become united with him in the likeness of His death certainly we shall be also in the likeness of His resurrection."*

In our human birth we were begotten of our earthly fathers as the result of his act of love with our human mothers. The decent of the believer into the watery grave of baptism after declaring his faith in the historically established fact that *"Jesus is the Christ, the only begotten Son of the living God,"* is typical of our being in our mother's womb. Rising out of the water is typical of our being born out of our mother's womb. In other words we were begotten of our fathers and born out of our mother's womb. It is a beautiful figure.

I listed Gary Howe last as he was one of the most outstanding young men that I had the privilege to baptize. He was an All American football player who helped lead the University of Colorado to a National Championship in 1990. After his baptism he immediately began witnessing his faith to other athletes and whoever he came into contact with. He traveled with me and witnessed his faith to churches where I was scheduled to hold special services as shown in the picture below. In the picture next to him are Paul and Kelly Stern. Paul was a good friend of Gary Howe and witnessed his baptism. He heard me read from the eighth chapter of Acts and the account of the conversion and baptism of the Etheopian Eunich. After hearing the Apostle Paul preach, he stopped Paul and asked, *"Here is water, why can't I be baptized?"* He was immediately baptized. After witnessing Gary Howe's baptism, Paul Stearn cried, "Here is water, why can't I be baptized?" I baptized both Paul and Kelly that same hour.

These pictures pretty much speak for themselves. As suggested earlier, they depict the greatest joy we experienced in our ministry through the years. The last picture shows one of the greatest joys of bringing people to Christ. It is of taking the "Good Confession" of Tera Bjorklund, a basketball star on the University of Colorado's women's basketball team. Hearing the "Good Confession" almost always brings a loud response from those present of clapping hands and praising the Lord.

When we baptized a ninety-year old man named Mr. Grieves, we asked him how he felt when he came up out of the water. He exclaimed, "I feel wonderful! I feel wonderful! I feel wonderful!" His response was natural as he realized the three wonderful things had just happened to him. First, he had all his past sins washed away, as the Psalmist declares, "As far as the east is from the west our sins are removed from us." Psalm 103: 12. Secondly, he received the indwelling of the Holy Sprit into His life. Acts 4:32 declares, "And we are witnesses of these things, and so is the Holy Spirit, whom God has given to those who obey Him." ALL THIS AND HEAVEN TOO! For the third thing he received was the promise of everlasting life. As the most often quoted Scripture in the Bible declares, *"For God so loved the world that He gave His Only Begotten Son, that who ever believes in Him shall have EVERLASTING LIFE,"* John 3: 16. And in one of the last epistles in the New Testament we have this declaration, *"and He Himself is the propitiation for our sins; and not for ours only, but also FOR THOSE OF THE WHOLE WORLD!"*

I had the privilege of baptizing one of the football stars from the University of Illinois football team. He was a very large man. The baptistery overflowed when I lowered him into the water. When I brought him up out of the water, Danny Beaver a long time missionary to the Philippine Islands, who was a member of our Fellowship Athletes at that time, cried, "Oh my! Oh my! Oh my!" as I witnessed that large athlete put on his "Jesus suit."

Share our joy as you view the pictures we share with you in conclusion of our journey with angels in Colorado in my fourth book *Love is like a Lizard*.

Lisa Graff

Some of the Men and Women Who Were
Baptized During Our Ministry
at the University of Colorado

Bill Everett

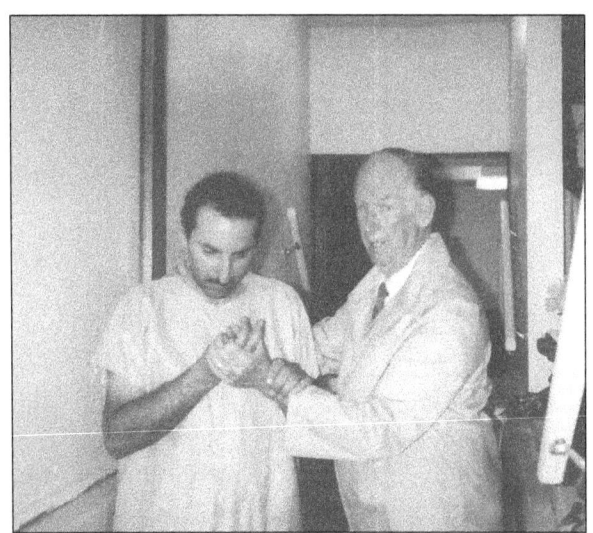

Reza Mahlouji

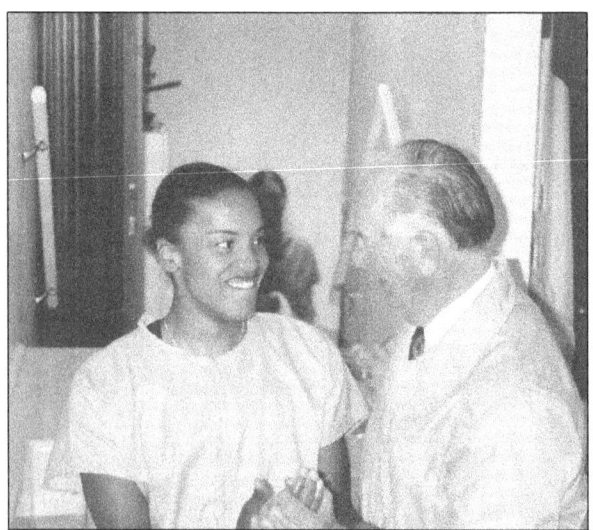

Di Spencer

Jamie Engelking

"*He that believeth and is baptized shall be saved.*"
—Mark 16:16

Carol Jahnlouji

Kelly Campbell

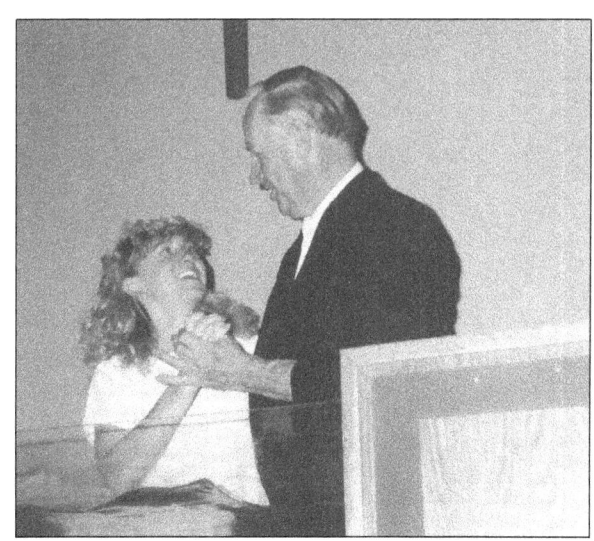

Kirston Everett

Julie Connelly

"*As many of you who have been baptzed into Christ have clothed yourselves with Christ.*"
—Galatians 3:27

Phil Dittberner

Sarah Leni

Tera Bjorklund

BIBLE QUIZ ANSWERS

1. True, Heaven and Earth, and man in his image.
2. True, Genesis 1:27.
3. False, Genesis 3:6.
4. True, Genesis 2: 22.
5. True, Genesis 2:7.
6. True, Genesis 1:20 living creatures (souls).
7. True, Genesis 1:3, (sun not placed in sky until Genesis 1:16, 17, 18).
8. True, Genesis 3:1-6.
9. False, the Indus River is in India.
10. True, Genesis 4:26.
11. True, Genesis 8:18.
12. True, there seemed to be a change in atmosphere that sped up the process of decay after the flood.
13. False, Elijah was taken up in a chariot, II Kings 2:11.
14. True.
15. True, Genesis 9:21
16. False.
17. False.
18. True.
19. True, 127 years old, Genesis 23:1.
20. True, they had the same father.
21. True, Mark and Luke are the other two.
22. True, Luke 3:38.
23. True, Matthew 17:3, on the Mount of Transfiguration.
24. True, Jesus' baptism, John's baptism, Great Commission baptism, Holy Spirit baptism, and baptism of suffering.
25. True, I Corinthians 13:13.

Books by Pearn and Associates, Inc.

Novels:

1945, Joseph J. Kozma, (fiction), paper *
Another Chance, Joe Naiman, (fiction — publisher only) cloth
Light Across the Alley, The Story of a Young Matchmaker,
    Victor W. Pearn (fiction) Kindle Books only*
Point Guard, Victor Pearn (fiction) cloth

Nonfiction:

Love is like a Lizard, Dr. Jerry Gibson, paper
A Lenten Journey Toward Christian Maturity, William E.
    Breslin (prayer guide, also available in Spanish) paper
Black 14: The Rise, Fall and Rebirth of Wyoming Football,
    Ryan Thorburn (sports biography) paper
Cowboy Up: Kenny Sailors, The Jump Shot and Wyoming's
    Championship Basketball History,
    Ryan Thorburn, (sports biography) paper †*
Dream Season, My Brother Gary and the 1957 Ashland Panthers
    Victor W. Pearn (sports biography) Kindle Books only*
Goulash and Picking Pickles, Louise Hoffmann (biography) cloth
Ikaria: A Love Odyssey on a Greek Island, Anita Sullivan
    (biography) paper *
I Look Around for my Life, John Knoepfle (biography) cloth*
It Started & Ended: **The Story About a Soldier and Civilian Life,**
    Bud Grounds (biography) paper
Lost Cowboys: The Bud Daniel Story, and Wyoming Baseball,
    Ryan Thorburn (sports biography) paper
The Great Adventure—UNTOLD, Charles Hamman, (nonfiction) cloth*

Poetry:

Mathematics in Color, Joseph J. Kozma (poetry) paper
The Dreamer and the Dream, Rick E. Roberts (poetry) paper
Until We Meet, Joseph J. Kozma (poetry) paper
Walking in Snow, John Knoepfle (poetry) paper

Available on Barnesandnoble.com
†Available on Nook; *Available on Kindle Books,
Amazon.com, (also available from Ingram Books, and Baker and Taylor,
you may order at your local bookstore
or directly from the publisher, happypoet@hotmail.com.

www.ingramcontent.com/pod-product-compliance
Lightning Source LLC
Chambersburg PA
CBHW062139160426
43191CB00014B/2335